The Smart Manager's
FAQ
Guide

The Smart Manager's FAQ Guide

A Survival Handbook for Today's Workplace

Rex P. Gatto

JOSSEY-BASS/PFEIFFER
A Wiley Company
San Francisco

ISBN: 0-7879-5344-X

Library of Congress Cataloging-in-Publication Data
Gatto, Rex P.
The smart manager's F.A.Q. guide : a survival handbook for today's
workplace / Rex P. Gatto.
     p. cm.
    Includes bibliographical references and index.
    ISBN 0-7879-5344-X (acid-free)
    1. Management. I. Title. II. Title: Smart manager's FAQ guide.
HD31.G368 2000
658—dc21   00-009154

Printed in the United States of America

Published by
JOSSEY-BASS/PFEIFFER
A Wiley Company
San Francisco
350 Sansome Street, 5th Floor
San Francisco, California 94104-1342
(415) 433-1740; Fax (415) 433-0499
(800) 274-4434; Fax (800) 569-0443

www.pfeiffer.com

Acquiring Editor: Matthew Holt
Director of Development: Kathleen Dolan Davies
Developmental Editor: Susan Rachmeler
Editor: Rebecca Taff
Senior Production Editor: Dawn Kilgore
Manufacturing Supervisor: Becky Carreño

Printing 10 9 8 7 6 5 4 3 2 1

 This book is printed on acid-free, recycled stock that meets or exceeds the minimum GPO and EPA requirements for recycled paper.

This book is dedicated to the hundreds of people we have worked with
to refine the tools presented in this book.
Thanks to my wife, Mickey, who worked tirelessly
with rewrites and creative thoughts.
She touched each page and made it better.
Thanks to Susan Rachmeler for her input.

IN MEMORY

Randall T. Cartwright

Patricia Fitzgibbons-Struttmann

Both taken at a very young age from the workplaces they loved.

Contents

Introduction

TODAY WE ARE DEFINING and redefining successful performance in the workplace. What was successful yesterday may not be of help today as we all try to outperform the clock—to do more with less in our increasingly fast-paced, impersonal workplace. This is cause for concern. In the 1990s, global competition was established as the norm. Competition from emerging democracies and growing economic powerhouses worldwide—and a new competitive surge within the United States—created and will re-create a new workplace. As organizations respond to and prepare for new economic, competitive, and technical changes through mergers, acquisitions, and reorganizations, this new workplace will continue to evolve and emerge.

The Smart Manager's FAQ Guide was written to support managers as they strive to deal with a variety of issues in an increasingly complex workplace. This book will help you build a strong foundation to meet the demands of your workplace. It outlines skills that are needed to succeed on the job, covering both business and self-development issues, such as problem solving and dealing with procrastination and anger.

To make the most effective use of the book, first review the table of contents. Listed alphabetically are all the topic areas covered. Under each topic are questions that you may find yourself asking on a daily basis. The "answers" provided in this book will help you successfully address work-related issues throughout the day. You can read this book cover to cover, but the book is best used as a reference tool—to meet the need for information as it arises. Just like a carpenter uses a saw, hammer, and nails to build a house, you can use the tools in this book to build your skills for addressing day-to-day business issues. The information is presented in an easy-to-use format to help you quickly address issues and take action in a positive and successful manner.

There is no one "right" way to address all the workplace problems or opportunities you encounter every day. This book is not a cure, but a tool box, filled with useful, practical ideas for reflection; techniques; and advice that can be used in conjunction with your own creative thinking.

Anger
Management

How Can I Deal with an Angry Employee?

ANGER IS AN UNFORTUNATE BY-PRODUCT of our fast-paced, quick-thinking, and results-oriented society. Time pressures, continual change, and unrealistic or changing expectations all fuel anger. We also put a lot of pressure on ourselves. When something prevents us from achieving our goals or infringes on our ability to function as we would like, anger may result. Because anger is counterproductive and potentially destructive, we need to find a way to address and resolve it. The Anger Model on the following page illustrates how anger begins and what we do with it.

Anger Model

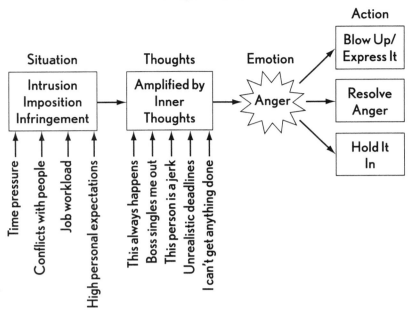

Thoughts That Fuel Anger

In addition to those shown in the model, the following types of thoughts may exacerbate an employee's anger. Be aware that these thoughts are not always rational or accurate, although the employee may believe they are.

- Blaming—should have/could have (My manager should have given me better directions. . . . I could have finished it if he had given me more details. . . . Every time I start this project, I am interrupted.)

- I am right (I know the client would have liked my way better, but my manager wanted it her way. . . . I've done this before just like this, and it worked!)

- Hopelessness or frustration (I just can't do it that way any longer. . . . I have tried and tried, but it just doesn't work for me. . . . I don't know what to do now. I am doing the work of three people. . . . My boss is always on the phone with personal calls.)

- Violated value (I knew I should have entered those cash payments, but the boss said not to worry about it, that no one would ever know. But I know. . . . The customer will know that the product doesn't meet the specifications, no matter what my boss says.)

Signs of Anger

Although you can't see the thoughts percolating, there are other visible signs that indicate that an employee may be angry:

- Protruding jaw,
- Clenched teeth,
- Tight neck and back muscles,
- Tightened fists,
- Trembling,
- Yelling or raised voice,
- Red face,
- Blotched face,
- Staring at someone, or
- Crying.

Responses to Anger

When someone expresses anger, listen without rebuttal; try to understand, rather than trying to think of a way to respond. Focus on identifying the problem. Once you think you have identified the problem, calmly and clearly paraphrase what the employee sees as the problem. By doing this, you acknowledge the issue. Please note that this does not mean that you have to agree with the employee; you are simply stating that you understand that the employee is angry about a given situation. ("You are angry about [specific problem]. Is that right?" or "You seem to be upset about [specific problem].")

Ask for and focus on agreement. State the problem as you see it, and then ask, "Can we agree that this is the problem?" Get the employee to state, "This is how I feel. I think that. . . ."

Sometimes you will have to wait until the person fully lets the anger out—which might include using vulgar language, making emotional statements, or expressing untrue or hostile thoughts or even hatred. By letting people vent their anger, you allow them to let off steam, thus dissipating the anger.

If possible, take a break. Go out of the room to get a soft drink or coffee. After five or ten minutes, return. To break the cycle of anger, it is important to intervene with facts and figures, not emotions. Refer back to the Anger Model above. You break the anger process by challenging thoughts, that is, by challenging the person's inner thoughts and focusing on a rational response. Listen, paraphrase, and share ideas. Don't let yourself become angry; when anger is met with anger, the situation only goes from bad to worse.

If the anger escalates, ensure that the employee is not going to harm himself or herself or others. Let the employee know that you are committed to talk through this with him or her. If you feel that the employee is still angry and hostile, protect yourself emotionally and physically by leaving the situation, and, if appropriate, calling security. In the case of escalated anger, you should note it in the employee's record, and include your actions also.

It is important for the employee to believe that he or she can do something to control the anger. One way to achieve this is to have the employee use the following questions and statements.

Preparing for Anger

- Are my thoughts factual or emotional?
- This could be a rough situation, but I know I can deal with it.

- I can work out a plan to handle this.
- I can stick to the issues and not take it personally.
- Relax, I am in charge of myself.
- There won't be any need for an argument. I know what to do.
- What am I thinking right now that is making me upset?

Impact and Confrontation

- I am ready for this event to begin.
- As long as I keep my cool, I'm in control of the situation.
- I don't need to prove myself. I won't make more out of this than I need to.
- I will not get into "I should/they should; I shouldn't/they shouldn't."

Afterthoughts

- What did I learn?
- How can I grow from this experience?
- I will focus on what happened. I will look for what was accomplished and give myself credit.
- I will focus on the positive.
- I will challenge my thoughts.
- I will not let negative thoughts interfere with my job or future meetings.
- I will be proactive in taking constructive and appropriate action.
- I will try to relax. I will use deep breathing and muscle tension/relaxation exercises.
- I will remember that, even though I may not have accomplished what I wanted, I am going to use this as a learning experience and preparation for the next situation.

Actions Against Anger

After you have defused an employee's anger, you can suggest the following techniques for anger management:

- Talk with someone who can help you understand why you are so angry.
- Write your ideas until there is nothing left to be said, reread them, and then challenge your thoughts.
- Recognize what is causing you to be angry.
- Don't avoid the emotion of anger; recognize and try to work through it.
- If you frequently become angry, learn to recognize early signs so you can seek help or discuss the issue early.
- Focus on acceptable outcomes, results, and positive action.
- Focus on solutions to problems.
- Develop a plan of action that focuses on positive energy and resolution.
- Use the list of questions and statements in the previous section to help you recognize and deal with anger.

As a manager, you can give the following scale to an employee who has had an "anger attack" and ask that he or she rate the level of personal anger. The higher the number, the more the employee has control of the anger. The lower the number, the more the anger has control of the employee. Ask the employee to use this each time he or she begins to feel anger. By doing this, the employee can learn to evaluate the level of his or her anger and use appropriate tools to deal with that anger.

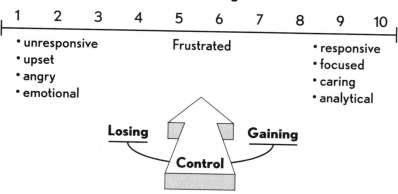

Rate Your Anger

1 2 3 4 5 6 7 8 9 10

- unresponsive
- upset
- angry
- emotional

Frustrated

- responsive
- focused
- caring
- analytical

Losing   Gaining

Control

Remember

- Sometimes anger is needed to clear the air and lead to a positive result.

- Anger is detrimental if unresolved; if resolved to everyone's satisfaction, it can strengthen a relationship.

- When a situation or event sparks anger, analyze it, the people involved, and the outcome you want to accomplish.

RESOURCES

Burns, D. (1989). *The feeling good handbook.* New York: Plume Books.

Ellis, A., & Lange, A. (1994). *How to keep people from pushing your buttons.* New York: Carol Publishing Group.

Freeman, A., & DeWolf, R. (1989). *Woulda coulda shoulda.* New York: Silver Arrow.

Freeman, A., Pretzer, J., Fleming, B., & Simon, K. (1991). *Clinical applications of cognitive therapy.* New York: Plenum.

London, T. (1991). *Managing anger.* Evanston, IL: Garfield.

Change

What Is
Change Leadership?

CHANGE LEADERSHIP is a model that uses a combination of leadership styles to keep employees and organizations ready for continual learning and growth. This style differs greatly from the traditional leadership model, which is geared toward control by the manager over the employee. Change leaders are people who think ahead, who know the destination, have the confidence within themselves to create change, and have the fortitude to help or redirect others to change also. We can't control change, but we can prepare for it.

A good manager uses different styles and skills at different times. The skills needed to lead an organization through change successfully are becoming increasingly important as the pace of change accelerates and affects more and more organizations. Change leaders need to know the good points and the faults of their own organizations, as well as those of other organizations.

Managers can become change leaders by the continual acquisition of knowledge, such as becoming aware of new theories in their field of business, learning to utilize new technologies, being able to adapt and adopt skills and strategies, and being open to creative thinking. Change leaders take advantage of their own talents and those of the people with whom they surround themselves. They need to know about technical workers (those who have specific knowledge) and knowledge workers (those who are generalists).

Change leaders are prepared for change, yet they are grounded in the traditions of organizational success. They create organizational stability and a sense of continuity, rather than using change for the sake of change, but are ready with the necessary knowledge when change and innovation are necessary. Change leaders realize that employees need to know:

- Where they are headed;
- What business they are in;
- With whom they will work;
- What is coming;
- What is expected of them;
- What will be valued;
- What the changes in procedure and process will be;
- How these changes will be measured;
- How their performance will be measured; and
- How the leaders themselves will model and accept change.

There are two foundations for building organizational change: *continuity* and *change*. Even though they appear to be diametrically opposite, they can, in fact, be complementary (Drucker, 1999). The key to balancing continuity and change is exceptional communication flow. One way to achieve this is as simple as a brief ten- to fifteen-minute meeting designed to put out information. Formal or informal, these meetings should be held at least once a week to inform, reassure, and support followers. Information should be "overshared" to show trust and keep people in the communication loop.

Create a New Mind-Set

By focusing on the future on such topics as changing markets, customer needs, or organizational restructuring, you will show others the way to build a successful organization. Here are some tips for developing a new way of thinking:

- Think about change, competition, and educated customer demands.
- Challenge your mind-set; expand your thinking.
- Deal with the situation as it is and develop alternatives. What do you want? What obstacles must you overcome?
- Listen attentively to issues, concerns, and ideas others provide.
- Approach the future as a beginning, not as a repetition of past events.
- Accept where you are and plan for the future. Do not put energy into "I should have."
- Utilize and build on your strengths as you plan.
- Realize that change involves risk taking and flexibility.
- Do not rationalize why you can't do something.
- Understand resistance: listen, paraphrase, and discuss.
- Create a clear vision and direction for everyone to follow.

Three Change Leadership Strategies

The following are three different leadership strategies for working through change. These can be used individually or combined.

1. Leading Change Through Power

In this style, the manager:

- Controls rewards, promotions, and advancements;
- Makes all decisions with little input from employees; and
- Is an autocratic/directing leader.

This leadership style can be effective during a crisis when a decision needs to be made quickly.

2. Leading Change Through Reason

In this style, the manager:

- Disseminates information prior to change;
- Treats employees like adults, explaining the "why" of the change; and
- Recognizes the motives, needs, traditions, and standards of the employees and the organization.

This leadership strategy is utilized when change is inevitable and time is not a factor.

3. Leading Change Through Re-Education

In this style, the manager:

- Realizes that neither power nor reason alone can bring about successful change;
- Values training and development;
- Encourages and allows employees to develop new skills for new challenges; and
- Motivates the employees to do more than is expected, pushes them beyond their level of confidence, and helps them to transcend self for the sake of the organization.

This strategy is effective in leading change during growth, rapid change, and strong competition.

RESOURCES

Argyris, C. (1973). *Intervention theory and method: A behavioral science view.* Reading, MA: Addison-Wesley.

Baron, R.A., & Greenberg, J. (1986). *Behavior in organizations.* Boston, MA: Allyn and Bacon.

Bass, B. (1985). *Leadership and performance beyond expectations.* New York: The Free Press.

Drucker, P. (1999). *Management challenges for the 21st century.* New York: Harper Business.

Gatto, R. (1992). *Teamwork through flexible leadership.* Pittsburgh, PA: GTA Press.

Gibson, J., Ivancevich, J., & Donnelly, J. (1997). *Organizations: Behavior, structure, processes.* Boston, MA: Irwin/McGraw-Hill.

What Is the Process of Change and Who Should Be Involved?

THE ABILITY TO CHANGE is an important part of the business environment. Every day, people are forced to adapt to circumstances beyond their control in order to be productive and successful. Some people do this better than others because of their organizational and interpersonal skills. The situation could be as minor as a telephone interruption or as major as assuming new job responsibilities.

The Road to Change

Organizations going through successful change need to focus on opportunities. To begin on the road to change, you first need to ask several questions:

- What needs to be improved?
- How will it be improved?
- What are the results to be achieved through improvement?

- How will the improvement process be implemented?
- What are the ramifications for the improvement?

Change Process

The following model can be used to help explain the change process. A description of the model follows.

Change Process

Present

Analyze the present situation. What led up to it? What is occurring now? What will be the outcome without change? What are the organizational standards and traditions?

Future Results

Identify needs, wants, and desires that will influence others to want change. Know the destination, the goal. Know the vision through understanding, reflection, intuition, and a sense of direction.

Strategy

How will you get where you want to go? Understand the "what" and the "how" needed to be accomplished to reach the destination. Will you go straight through or change in the middle? Strategy cannot be implemented without having a clear understanding of future results.

Transformational Action

Know the actions that are to be implemented and measured to ensure that each step or phase of the strategy is accomplished. These are the day-to-day actions of the major plan. This is what puts the strategy in place and holds people accountable.

Reassess

When you arrive, do you know where you are? Did you achieve the results you wanted? Measure what the strategy and transformation did for the organization.

This model is useful to managers in identifying which step of the change process they are in. It also allows them to see what comes next.

Roles Within the Change Process

A variety of people may be involved in the change process, including the following:

- *Change Advocate* (could be upper management or manager): Group or person who has identified the need for change, has the reasons and strategies for change, but does not have the authority to legitimize change.

- *Change Sponsor:* Decision maker who has the authority to legitimize change; one sponsor could involve others.

- *Change Agent:* Person or group who acquires the appropriate involvement and commitment of sponsors and is responsible for planning and implementing change.

- *Change Target:* Group/department/division/person who need(s) to adopt and use the concepts supported in the change process; one group's change could lead to another group's change.

Criteria for Implementing Change

Before beginning the change process, four criteria must be met:

1. A direction/result must be identified.
2. People must know that staying in the present is more painful than reaching out to achieve the results.
3. An implementation and measurement system or strategy must be found to close the gap between the present and the desired future.
4. The skills and resources needed to close the gap must be realistic and attainable.

The following acronym can help you to remember some of the issues relevant to change:

Courage to risk, ask, challenge, and meet future needs.

Have an understanding of self and others.

Analyze the general and specific terms.

Need to know, research, develop and concur.

Go with your greatest strengths.

Expected results should be identified.

RESOURCES

Abernathy, D.J. (1999, March). Leading edge learning: Interviews with Peter Senge and John H. Welch, Jr. *Training & Development,* pp. 40–42.

Bennis, W., & Nanus, B. (1985). *Leaders: The strategy for taking charge.* New York: Harper and Row.

Greenberg, J. (1999). *Managing behavior in organizations* (2nd ed.). Upper Saddle River, NJ: Prentice Hall.

Peters, T. (1987). *Thriving on chaos.* New York: Knopf.

Senge, P.M. (1990). *The fifth discipline.* New York: Doubleday.

Q How Can I Handle Resistance to Change?

"Successful resistance is the ability to avoid getting what you don't want from yourself, others, and the environment."

H.B. Karp

WHEN PEOPLE THINK OF CHANGE, they automatically project how it will affect them personally. In the workplace, employees can have a great resistance to change. To influence the employees effectively, you will have to overcome this resistance. Biases, comforts, and traditional ways will have to be addressed as you sell your ideas. Employee resistance may be caused by any of the following:

- Previous successes; if people have been successful in the past, they may not want to change to an unknown future;
- A feeling of familiarity with the way things are;
- A sense of safety and security; or
- A level of confidence that has been reinforced by tradition, standards, and competitors.

As you begin to influence for change, remember:

- All new concepts eventually become outdated, so in order to succeed, you will need to develop alternatives, adaptations, and innovations.

- Creativity and problem solving will help you meet future needs. As the future cannot be controlled, you must be ready to adapt to unexpected occurrences.

The following model (Karp, 1985) identifies some reasons why people resist change. The victims and losers in the model may move to being resistors if they want a sense of power. Think about the resistors. If resistors are successful, they become winners and achieve a sense of power. Thus, resistors, by achieving this sense of power, can influence other employees and create a real block to change.

Power/Resistance Model

	I Want	I Don't Want
I Get	Winner (Power)	Victim
I Don't Get	Loser	Resistor (Resistance)

adapted from H.B. Karp, 1985

The keys to dealing with resistance and eliminating blocks to change include the following:

- Honor differing viewpoints;
- Look for areas of agreement;
- Be open and flexible to new ideas; and
- Identify areas of conflict and problem solve.

By honoring others' viewpoints, looking for agreement, and being open, you can include the resisting employee in the decision-making process and can change the resistance power into participatory power through problem solving.

RESOURCES

Gatto, R., (1992). *Teamwork through flexible leadership.* Pittsburgh, PA: GTA Press.

Karp, H.B. (1985). *Personal power: An unorthodox guide to success.* New York: American Management Association.

Kotter, J.P. (1996). *Leading change.* Cambridge, MA: Harvard Business School Press.

Smith, D.K. (1996). *Taking charge of change.* Reading, MA: Addison-Wesley.

Cognitive Processes

Q How Can I Counteract Negativity?

MANY PEOPLE IN THE WORKPLACE have irrational thoughts—known as *cognitive distortions*—and then take action based on them. These cognitive distortions lead to negative thoughts, as shown in the table below. One of the major problems is that negativity can limit a person's creativity and can hamper cooperation and positive relationships with co-workers. Employees' thoughts drive their level of productivity, efficiency, motivation, and interpersonal rapport. If you, as a manager, notice that an employee is frequently voicing negative thoughts like those in the following list, you can counter the negative statements with corresponding positive ones.

Cognitive Distortion	Thoughts
All or Nothing There is only one way to do this correctly.	**Negative Thought** "I have too much to do."
	Positive Thought Look for alternatives; be flexible; break projects into smaller, more manageable assignments; stop looking at things in black-and-white terms, focusing on the bad while overlooking the good; a small failure does not discount all the good.
Overgeneralization One bad decision or action means everything will go wrong.	**Negative Thought** "I can't do anything right."
	Positive Thought Analyze the situation or action on its own terms; don't apply it to anything else.
Ruminating Dwelling on a negative event or statement, for example, in a performance appraisal focusing on the one "bad" statement and disregarding all of the positive and supportive statements.	**Negative Thought** "I can't believe he thinks I worry too much."

Cognitive Distortion	Thoughts
	Positive Thought
	Focus on the balance between what you have done right and what you need to improve; review your achievements.
Jumping to Conclusions	**Negative Thought**
Everything is screwed up; it's all wrong.	"I know what everyone thinks of me; they think I'm stupid."
	Positive Thought
	Ask questions; discuss a problem; don't assume the worst.
Using Emotional Rather than Rational Thinking	**Negative Thought**
Letting emotions get the better of you.	"I might get fired." "I feel rotten about this, therefore it must be bad." "I don't have the confidence to do this, therefore I am a poor employee."
	Positive Thought
	Don't create mental barriers and then justify your thinking. Remember why you have been successful.
Labeling	**Negative Thought**
Using a label to explain away problems or issues.	"I am a total failure." "Thisentire company stinks." "There is nothing good about any of these employees."

Cognitive Distortion	Thoughts
	Positive Thought People with different talents, approaches, and qualities run companies; labeling leads to stress, frustration, and anger. Focus on issues and on taking corrective action; find the right situation for you.
Personalizing Making yourself the center of all that is good or bad, focusing on the bad.	**Negative Thought** "This employee who reports to me is a failure; this shows I am a bad manager, even though ten other employees succeed."
	Positive Thought Quit blaming yourself for circumstances out of your control; stop feeling guilty, ashamed, and inadequate; look at what you have accomplished.
Should Have Wishful thinking after the fact.	**Negative Thought** "I should have thought about this before it happened." "I shouldn't have made this mistake."
	Positive Thought Reflect on "should have's" and the power they hold on you; break away from "I should" and replace with "I did"; use should, could, ought, and would sparingly.

Cognitive Distortion	Thoughts
Grass Is Greener Someone else does it better than you; someplace else is better than where you are now.	**Negative Thought** "Everyone else in my job was promoted before me." "Everyone else is more successful." **Positive Thought** The grass may be greener on the other side, but you still have to cut it; don't compare—there are many variables and uncontrolled issues; enjoy what you have; there will always be something you don't have.
Discounting the Positive Being self-critical	**Negative Thought** "I have a great position, but it really doesn't mean anything." **Positive Thought** Enjoy what you have accomplished.

RESOURCES

Burns, D. (1989). *The feeling good handbook.* New York: Plume Books.

Ellis, A., & Lange, A. (1994). *How to keep people from pushing your buttons.* New York: Carol Publishing Group.

Freeman, A., Pretzer, J., Fleming, B., & Simon, K. (1991). *Clinical applications of cognitive therapy.* New York: Plenum Press.

May, R. (1989). *The art of counseling.* New York: Gardner Press.

Q How Can I Avoid Procrastination?

IN THE WORKPLACE, procrastination takes away from efficiency, productivity, and organizational interaction. In some instances it becomes paralyzing, preventing people from taking action.

The following spoken statements or thoughts are signs of procrastination:

- I'll put it off until tomorrow.
- There isn't enough time.
- I have to do this first.
- This is a major problem; it can't be solved now. I can't solve it.
- This is too complex; I don't know where to begin.
- I don't have to do it now; I have a lot of time to finish. I'll do it later.
- What's the use? Why start?
- This is dumb, boring, and stupid.

What are the reasons behind procrastination? Not having the confidence to complete the work is one. Procrastinators believe that if they take no action, they cannot fail. Setting expectations too high is another. Perfectionism sometimes is the hidden reason behind procrastination: "If I can't do it perfectly, why do it at all?" Fear of being punished for *not* acting can sometimes stop procrastination: for example, concern about a poor performance rating if a project is not complete may motivate someone to begin that project. Fear, however, may not be enough to overcome procrastination. Following is a list of some more proactive techniques for reducing procrastination.

Techniques to Overcome Procrastination

1. Break large projects or assignments into smaller parts. For example, break down a performance appraisal for an employee this way:

   Meet with the employee Wednesday from 1 to 2 p.m.

   Write the performance appraisal Thursday starting at 3 p.m.

   Proofread and correct the performance appraisal Monday morning.

   Meet with the employee Wednesday at 10 a.m. to discuss strengths and developmental opportunities.

   Procrastination is about immediate enjoyment—do this rather than that. By setting a schedule, you can begin to eliminate procrastination's hold on you.

2. Another helpful way to overcome procrastination is to identify the benefits of accomplishing the task you have been putting off. For example, if you finish writing the report, you won't have to worry about it any longer; you can move on to more enjoyable tasks; you will finish the project, which could lead to an advancement; and so on.

3. Reward yourself for what you accomplish. For example, plan to do something special (go to the movies, eat ice cream) after completing a task.

4. Challenge yourself. Tell yourself that you CAN, in fact, do the task, that you know you have done it in the past. Focus on the task at hand and, when you become sidetracked, tell yourself that you know you are sidetracked and you will go back on task NOW.

5. The next time you find yourself procrastinating, try the following model and then use your responses to challenge yourself to begin whatever you have been putting off.

Procrastination Action Model

Advantage of Taking Action	Disadvantage of Taking Action
Advantage of Not Taking Action	Disadvantage of Not Taking Action

RESOURCES

Burns, D. (1989). *The feeling good handbook*. New York: Plume Books.

Ellis, A., & Lange, A. (1994). *How to keep people from pushing your buttons*. New York: Carol Publishing Group.

Freeman, A., & DeWold, A. (1989). *Woulda coulda shoulda*. New York: Silver Arrow.

What Can I Learn from a Failed Effort?

A FAMOUS STORY is told about Alfred Sloan, the automotive and business leader, who conceived the concept of decentralization. When a vice president submitted his resignation because of a costly mistake, Sloan ripped up the resignation, stating, "I just paid a lot of money to educate you." Failure is an education. Successful people fail more often because they try to accomplish more. Examining the causes of failure eliminates mistakes the next time around and allows you to look at alternatives. Those alternatives can lead to a positive and creative solution to the problem at hand.

Ask yourself the following questions, which can help you and your employees turn failure into a learning experience:

1. What results were you expecting? What actually occurred?

2. In planning, did you consider all possible obstacles?

3. Can the problem be rectified? Is the entire project doomed?

4. Did you collect input from the right people, ask the right questions?

5. What can be salvaged? Many problems can be resolved, although many people quit rather than work toward a solution.

6. Do you know when to stop or revamp?

7. What have you learned? How can you grow from this experience? What will you do differently? Did you learn anything from this experience?

From Failure to Success

In the mid-1970s, American Eagle Outfitters (AE) was launched as an active, outdoor retail store for men. The Pittsburgh-based retail chain sold clothing, tents, freeze-dried food, canoes, and gear. AE management built a successful retail chain over a short period of several years. In the late 1980s, the chain began a severe decline, and a series of leadership changes took place. The newest management was trying to reclaim the glory of the previous years by doing the same thing, only better, so they thought, with promotions, sales, lower prices, and so on. The problem was that it WAS the same old thing, simply with a different spin. The world and the customers had changed, and AE was standing still. By 1990, the company had lost close to $20 million. The early success of AE was, unfortunately, slipping into a decline.

In the early 1990s, new ownership and management with fresh ideas took over. This new management team developed a strategy that began by restoring basic, sound, business practices. They then went public and began the long climb to "re-success" by assembling a solid management group who created and were committed to a shared vision of a newly defined and continually redefined American Eagle, which could survive and grow in the changing marketplace.

The new management created a team comprised of all parts of the organization: merchandise, marketing, stores, finance, employees, real estate, service, product, music, training, and so on. The team researched opportunities, defined its target customer, and set the foundation for the brand strategy. That team continues to define and redefine strategies within the specific brand strategy. These steps have resulted in the explosive success that American Eagle has today, which includes its own magazine, credit card, website, and CD, all of which help to bring service to its customers.

American Eagle continues to be a major success story in retail. It has demonstrated that a solid business strategy, visionary management, and a keen eye on the customer can turn a declining retail chain into an American success story.

RESOURCES

Burns, D. (1989). *The feeling good handbook.* New York: Plume Books.

Ellis, A., & Lange, A. (1994). *How to keep people from pushing your buttons.* New York: Carol Publishing Group.

Freeman, A., & DeWold, R. (1989). *Woulda coulda shoulda.* New York: Silver Arrow.

Freeman, A., Pretzer, J., Fleming, B., & Simon, K. (1991). *Clinical applications of cognitive therapy.* New York: Plenum Press.

 # Communication

Q

What Different Techniques Can Be Used in Conversation?

PEOPLE INTERACT DIFFERENTLY because of the different approaches they take during a conversation. Some people have a single technique for communicating, while others use a variety of techniques. The more techniques you can utilize, the greater your chances of communicating effectively. The following lists the benefits of a number of communication techniques.

Technique	Example	Benefit(s)
Pausing	Silence	Emphasizes or clarifies a point of view. Slows the communication process.
Explaining	Describes something. Expresses a point of view. Disseminates	Presents one's thoughts and feelings. Creates a mutual understanding.

Technique	Example	Benefit(s)
	information. Presents facts and emotions. "The facts are. . . ." "The customer wants. . . . "	
Paraphrasing	Restate or rephrase what the speaker has said. "Did I understand you to say. . . ." "Your point is that. . . ."	Lets the speaker know you heard and understood what was said. Gives the speaker the opportunity to add or clarify ideas.
Questioning	Solicits a clarifi-cation. Expands an idea. Asks who, what, why, when, where. "Would you explain further?"	Explains and clar-ifies an idea. Achieves a better understanding.
Listening	Eye contact, head nod, facial expression, and an intangible connection. "I hear (see) what you are saying."	Shows respect. Gains a mutual understanding. Demonstrated through follow-up action.
Feeling	Expresses an opinion in terms of how I/we feel. Gives a point of reference other than just facts. "I feel that. . . ."	Gives an under-standing on an emotional level. Helps to under-stand how the speaker feels about the topic.

Technique	Example	Benefit(s)
	"My feeling is. . . ."	
Reinforcing	Supports an idea. Shows support. "I agree with that because. . . ."	Lets others know your ideas.
Relating	Tells a story. Relates an experience. "The last time we did this. . . ." "The customer told me they used. . . ." "What happened to us was. . . ."	Relaxes a conversation with a supporting story or experience. Shares personal experience. Builds rapport. Teaches.
Challenging	Indicates intellectual disagreement. Gives opposing view point stated professionally. "I see it differently." "I challenge the notion that. . . ." "That is not the way I see it."	Shows a differing point of view. States a different perspective, often a slight variation.
Humor	Smiles, jokes (but be careful!). Relates humorous or funny stories in a professional manner. "A funny thing happened on my way to work."	Breaks the ice. Breaks the tension.

Technique	Example	Benefit(s)
Interjecting	Interrupts in a professional manner. "Excuse me but the point is. . . ." "Let me interrupt."	Clarifies a point of view. Clarifies facts.
Attacking	Attacks verbally. "That is a stupid idea."	Shows the speaker's level of frustration or emotion.

RESOURCES

Alessandra, T., & Hunksaker, P. (1993). *Communication at work.* New York: Fireside.

Ellis, A. (1994). *How to keep people from pushing your buttons.* New York: Carol Publishing Group.

Gatto, R. (1991). *A practical guide to effective presentation.* Pittsburgh, PA: GTA Press.

How Can I Persuade People to Listen to Me?

WE HEAR, BUT DO WE LISTEN? Communication involves not only putting out information, but also taking in information. Listening is an important skill that can be refined to improve your communication. The benefit to effective listening in the workplace is efficiency of performance and less repetition. Listening is a communication connection, similar to shaking hands. When two people shake hands, there is a tangible connection. Listening is an intangible connection, focused on creating a mutual understanding. That understanding can establish performance goals and expectations.

The following is a list of reasons people use for not listening. Do any of these sound familiar?

- I don't have time.
- We're just going over the same old stuff.
- He/she is just complaining.
- I'm too fed up/too tired.
- I'm not interested.

- I have something else to do.
- I don't like or trust the speaker.
- This is a waste of time; I have better things to do.
- There's nothing in this for me.
- I disagree with the speaker.
- I don't value the information.
- I don't think the information is accurate.

People's listening is also affected by filters, factors such as their own knowledge or beliefs and values, as shown below.

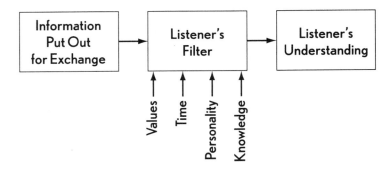

It is important to be able to overcome the reasons for not listening if you want to be able to listen to others and to help people listen to you in turn. Just because you say something, there is no guarantee that the listener hears, understands, feels the same way you do, or is capable of discussing it (or even wants to). Assume nothing in a conversation. You must ask questions to learn whether the listener understands what you're saying.

Sending Information to the Listener

To influence others effectively, you must consider numerous variables: people, information, the time, place, and circumstances. Here are some guidelines to help you persuade others to listen to what you have to say.

- Know the goal. What is to be accomplished?
- Identify the listener's needs by listening carefully and asking questions.
- Express the benefits for the listener ("What this means for you is. . . "). Relate business examples or success stories.
- Express your ideas at the level of and in the terms of the listener, not your own.
- Show competence and confidence.
- Be open, honest, respectful, and trusting.
- Establish the right time and place to meet.
- Measure the results.

The Three A's of Communication

When conducting a conversation, be aware of the three A's: *acquire, acknowledge,* and *act.*

Acquire

1. Find the right person; ask the right questions.
2. Collect information tactfully.
3. Ask general questions, then specific questions.
4. Listen; paraphrase.

Acknowledge

1. Identify the person's needs, wants, and expectations by listening and asking questions. State your understanding.
2. Identify what you expect to happen next.
3. Recap the process verbally and in writing (if appropriate) to the other person.

Act

1. Implement a process to achieve satisfaction.
2. Guide others at their own pace; build trust.

3. Continually reassess the process.

4. Follow up verbally or in writing (if appropriate).

Sample Discussion Using the Three A's

The following is a sample discussion between a manager and a group of salespeople using the three A's of communication described above.

Manager: (Acquire) Before we can really develop a strategy to work with Company A, we need to outline what we want to accomplish. Which people know what the company needs? Joe and Pat, you have worked closely with Company A. What are the goals/results they are looking for?

Joe: (Acquire) Delivery of the quality resins on time at a competitive price. To work with them as a preferred vendor.

Manager: (Acquire) What is their timetable for delivery? Can we meet it? At what price can we sell our products and still maintain a profit margin?

Pat: (Acquire) We can sell at a 15 percent markup and maintain the suggested corporate profit margin.

Manager: (Acknowledge) Let's see. I heard you say that Company A wants us to be a preferred vendor and that we can sell at a 15 percent markup. Could we do this with other customers?

Pat: (Acknowledge) That might be something we could offer Company D.

Manager: (Acknowledge) Let's do this. First, outline a plan for Company A. Second, review the plan to see whether we can offer that plan to other customers. Third, begin this sales rollout by first quarter. I'll write this up and send each of you a copy. I want feedback at our next meeting.

Manager: (Act) In summary, we have outlined what Cus-
            tomer A wants and will develop a plan of
            action. Maybe this plan could be used with
            other customers.

RESOURCES

Borisoff, D., & Victor, D.A. (1998). *Conflict management: A communication skills approach.* Boston, MA: Allyn and Bacon.

Gatto, R. (1990). *A practical guide to effective presentation.* Pittsburgh, PA: GTA Press.

Gatto, R. (1992). *Teamwork through flexible leadership.* Pittsburgh, PA: GTA Press.

Gibson, J., Ivancevich, J., &. Donnelly, J. (1997). *Organizations: Behavior, structure, processes.* Boston, MA: Irwin/McGraw-Hill.

Q How Can I Better Prepare for Phone Calls?

MORE AND MORE BUSINESS DISCUSSIONS are taking place over the telephone. In order to make effective use of your time, it is just as important to prepare for a phone call as it is to prepare for a face-to-face meeting. The next time you must place or return an important phone call, use the following format to help organize your ideas.

Project Name: _____

Caller's Name: _____

Office Phone: _____ Home Phone: _____

Purpose of the call: _____

Communication style, if known (blunt, influencing, detailed, sincere):

Concerns:

Comments:

What does the client need to be satisfied?

Notes on the conversation:

Below is an example of a telephone worksheet that has been filled in.

Project Name: ___The Landmarks File___

Caller's Name: ___Elizabeth Brown___

Office Phone: ___222-333-7474___ Home Phone: ___NA___

Purpose of the call: ___Discuss the proposed time frame.___

Communication style, if known (blunt, influencing, detailed, sincere):
___Detailed and sincere.___

Concerns:
___Time frame is too tight. Can we add a week in the middle?___
___What happens if we run over?___

Comments:

What does the client need to be satisfied?
___Ask!___

Notes on the conversation:

When talking on the phone, remember the following points:

- Ask questions, going from general to specific.
- Use open probes: How? What? Why?
- Influence by listening first and then responding.
- Identify agreement and concerns.
- Listen.
- Summarize.
- Always take good notes so you'll have an accurate record of your conversation.

RESOURCES

Gatto, R. (1990). *A practical guide to effective presentation.* Pittsburgh, PA: GTA Press.

Learning Annex. (1994). *How to win on the telephone.* New York: Berkeley Books.

How Can I Write More Effective E-Mails?

ELECTRONIC MAIL IS COMMONPLACE in the business world, but not everyone takes full advantage of this medium. Many people dash off unclear, incomplete, or confusing e-mail messages, thus short-circuiting the communication process. E-mail is a powerful tool that, when used appropriately, can make communication much easier. Next time you prepare to write an e-mail, use the following format to prepare a draft and, in the future, be sure all your e-mails cover these important points.

Subject Line (be specific and clear):

_____

_____

Purpose of the e-mail (brief overview):

_____

_____

What is to be accomplished (brief statement):

_____

_____

_____

_____

_____

Topic (bullet points):

_____

_____

_____

_____

_____

Response timeframe:

_____

_____

_____

The following is an example of a filled-out e-mail worksheet:

Subject Line (be specific and clear):

Meeting, September 12, 2:10 p.m.

Purpose of the e-mail (brief overview):

Meeting to discuss new product advertising

What is to be accomplished (brief statement):

Brainstorm
Choose direction
Set timeframe

Topic (bullet points):

Approach to take
Agencies to use

Response timeframe:

Indicate availability by September 1

As you write your e-mails, keep the following points in mind:

- Write your comments from general to specific.
- Use open probes. Ask how, what, why.
- Identify what you assume to be agreement and concerns.
- Summarize and identify follow-up action.
- Sign your e-mail.

RESOURCES

Gatto, R. (1990). *A practical guide to effective presentation.* Pittsburgh, PA: GTA Press.

Learning Annex. (1994). *How to win on the telephone.* New York: Berkeley Books.

Ludden, L., & Capozzoli, T. (2000). *Supervisor savvy.* Indianapolis, IN: JIST Works.

How Can I Use Different Styles to Communicate Effectively?

HOW WELL YOU COMMUNICATE is demonstrated when you express your thoughts, both verbally and nonverbally. There are basically two ways to communicate—through actions or through words. Effective communication may close information gaps, create a clear and mutual understanding, build trust, monitor performance, and indicate vision or direction. The ability to communicate, however, is altered (for better or worse) by the people you are speaking with, by the environment, and by time pressures. To communicate effectively, it is necessary to understand the different communication styles and when to use which one.

Four Styles of Communication

To communicate most effectively, it is essential that you be able to use different communication styles. You should be flexible enough to meet the needs of the situation and the listener(s).

For example, at times, people may need long discussions, while at other times a brief explanation will suffice. A description of the four basic communication styles follows.

Blunt, Aggressive, Take-Charge Style

With this style, the speaker is in charge and likes to be challenged. The speaker tends to be brief and is frequently a poor listener who wants quick results. The effective aggressive communicator dispenses with information quickly and responds to questions quickly. Some people may assume that a person with this style is uncaring and impersonal. Poor listening may result because this type usually goes on to another thought and/or is quick to respond or rebut ideas without letting others finish their statements. If you think you use this style to excess, you need to concentrate on what your listeners are saying. You may want to take notes to collect information accurately and to avoid responding too quickly.

Influencing, Persuading Style

The person who uses this style likes to be popular and also talks a great deal. This effective style gives a lot of information; however, the question is, "Is it all needed?" If you use this particular style a great deal of the time, you must learn to prepare so that you know exactly what you want to say. Do not repeat or over-sell every idea. Create a structure by writing notes or an agenda, and then stick to it. Don't embellish or editorialize.

Sincere, Sensitive, Kind-Hearted Style

This style sounds sincere to others, and the person usually likes to be a team player. The person using this style may desire a lot of personal attention, but also gives a lot. This speaker is generally turned off by aggressiveness. If you are this kind of communicator, remember that not everyone needs the same sense of belonging or affiliation as you do.

Detailed, Logical, Analytical Style

Speakers who use this style are generally thorough and like low risks. A person with this style puts out a great deal of information and is logical, detail-oriented, and likes to ponder. This type of speaker leaves little information out of the communication. However, the question is, "Does everyone need to hear everything?" If you use this style a great deal, try to simplify what you say. At times, you may have to provide the big picture instead of so much detail. Too many details often confuse the issue instead of clarifying it.

The most effective communication style is a *balance* of all four styles. To communicate effectively and have the greatest influence on others, first ask yourself what is appropriate for the situation. Adapt your style of communicating to the listeners.

RESOURCES

Gatto, R. (1990). *A practical guide to effective presentation.* Pittsburgh, PA: GTA Press.

Gatto, R. (1999). *My preferred style of communication inventory.* Pittsburgh, PA: GTA Press.

Gibson, J., Ivancevich, J., & Donnelly, J. (1997). *Organizations: Behavior, structure, processes.* Boston, MA: Irwin/McGraw-Hill.

Myers-Briggs, I. (1980). *Gifts differing.* Palo Alto, CA: Consulting Psychologists Press.

Tannen, D. (1995). *Talking 9 to 5.* New York: Avon.

How Can I Best Respond to Questions?

MAKING SURE YOU UNDERSTAND what the other person is saying is an especially important aspect of communication. Also, you must be sure that the person understands you. Asking and answering questions is a way to clarify and improve two-way understanding. It's important to show that you are interested when you answer someone's question. Make eye contact and nod your head to indicate that you understand what the person says. Use the following steps to make sure you respond to questions appropriately.

1. Listen to the terms of the questions. Were the terms (concepts) specific or general?

   Specific (analytical): Give analytical, detailed, or data-supported answers.

   General (big picture, global): Answer with exploring, sensitive, suggestive, or all-encompassing terms.

2. Listen to how the question is asked. Listen for visual, verbal, and/or feeling cues.

Visual: "Do you see what I mean?"

Aural: "Doesn't that say something about . . . ?"

Emotional: "Don't you feel that. . . ?"

3. Address the questions in the same mode as they are asked.

Visual: "I see what you are saying"; "I imagine. . . ."; "I look. . . ."; "In my mind's eye. . . ."; "My view-point is. . . ."

Aural: "I hear what you are saying."; "I'll tell you."; "I am attuned to. . . ."; "Let me reiterate."; "In response to. . . ."

Emotional: "I feel. . . ."; "My gut feeling is. . . ."; "Emotionally I agree. . . ."; "You can reach. . . ."

If you are confused or need to have a point clarified, interject or ask a question. Do not let the discussion continue. The other party assumes that there is mutual understanding if you continue without interruption.

4. When someone asks a question for which you do not readily have an answer, listen attentively (make eye contact and acknowledge). Ask a question in return. This will give you more time to think of an appropriate response. For example:

Why do you ask that?

That is a very interesting thought; could you expand on your idea?

What do you think the ramifications of that would be?

How do you think that could be accomplished?

5. If you do not know an answer to a question:

State that you do not know.

Emphasize the resources you have available for finding the answer (research, data, personnel, networking system, etc.).

Let questioner know you will follow up and get back to him or her.

Set a time for follow-up discussion.

Remember that listening is more important than responding, and that your answers should always be focused on the question.

RESOURCES

Argyris, C. (1991). Teaching smart people how to learn. *Harvard Business Review, 69*(3), 99-109.

Gatto, R. (1990). *A practical guide to effective presentation.* Pittsburgh, PA: GTA Press.

Gibson, J., Ivancevich, J., & Donnelly, J. (1997). *Organizations: Behavior, structure, processes.* Boston, MA: Irwin/McGraw-Hill.

Ludden, L., & Capozzoli, T. (2000). *Supervisor savvy.* Indianapolis, IN: JIST Works.

How Can I Influence Others to Adopt My Ideas?

INFLUENCE IS THE INTERACTION between and among people that causes change or encourages support of a concept. It results in a unity and clarification when there might have been diversity or conflict. Influence causes a union of thought—possibly through give-and-take—and adoption or adaptation of ideas. To influence, there must be a willingness to trust, listen, accept, reflect, discuss, and take action. This process takes time. However, the benefit of exerting influence is that it can create consistency and high levels of focused productivity.

How to Influence

The actions listed below could be used in various orders. Try them when you need to influence others.

- Establish a *safe environment* that fosters a sharing of ideas and builds rapport (acceptance) and trust. For example, do not put down employees' ideas. Always be positive. ("That's a good thought.")

- Explain *purpose, expected results,* and *level of importance.* ("We are here to look at new ways to distribute our product. We hope to have a more timely system in place by next year.")
- Establish *direction* (business objectives, desired results, outcomes) and topics to be discussed. ("We will talk about where we should be in three years and how we will get there.")
- Establish a *plan of action* and *procedures* and implement that process; establish a *time frame.* ("We will begin by asking each department to explain. . . .")
- Develop *alternatives*; be flexible and able to deal with change. Listen and discuss ideas openly. Share your positional power, prestige, influence, authority; involve everyone. ("We have called this general meeting so that each of you can have input into how we should begin to restructure.")
- Listen effectively; seek to *understand* others first, then communicate. Try to comprehend other peoples' ideas to establish a mutual understanding. ("So, what you are saying is. . . . ")
- Come to an *agreement.* Discuss ideas. Clarify your understanding. ("I see. I think we both want the same thing, which is. . . .")
- Establish a *climate* in which people will become ready to believe in and accept what is said and be influenced, as well as influence others. ("As we have done in the past, we WILL take your ideas into consideration.")

The Influence Process in Action

This process is a tool to measure the changing relationships among people. It should be used as a flexible guideline to influence others. The process is based on a commonsense approach for listening, asking the right questions, responding, and focusing on agreeing to take action. Many people may do this naturally. This is not a quick fix, but it is a process to guide you and others.

Ask yourself the following questions before you prepare to try to influence someone:

Preparation Questions

- What is the goal?
- What issues must be addressed?
- What is the presentation strategy: facts and figures, or intuition and support?
- How can I phrase the issue, problem, or goal to have a significant influence on the listener? (If the person is creative and intuitive, stress the possibilities. If he or she is practical, develop a step-by-step plan for working. If he or she is action-oriented, put dates and a timetable in your action plan.)

Use the Model for Influencing shown below and the following examples to help yourself prepare to exert influence.

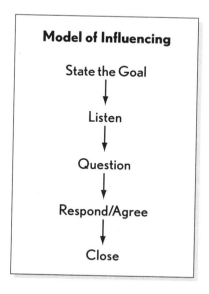

The following is an example of using influence in an internal meeting to standardize the way a company calls on customers.

Initial Discussion—State the Goal

- The goal is to establish guidelines using a standardized format to better meet the client needs.
- The feedback received through customer surveys indicates that our company is not consistent from department to department while working with clients.
- What do you think we need to do differently?
- What can we do to develop consistent guidelines?

Focus on Needs—Listen

- What is our goal when working with clients?
- What do our customers really want in our products or services?
- Who are our customers' competitors?
- How involved should management be in addressing customer complaints?

Identify Issues—Question

- Ask the following questions:
  - How does management propose to address issues?
  - When is the process to be in place?
  - When will the customer assessment be completed?
  - Are we consistent in identifying how customers evaluate our products and services?
  - Are we helping our customers compete in the market?
  - What are the benefits to this process?

Achieve an Understanding—Respond/Agree

- What problems do you see with this process?
- How does this sound to you?

Summary—Close

- The process will be up to you to develop and implement.
- What do we agree on?
- What is your level of commitment?

Using this influencing process will help you have a positive impact on others. It will guide you to achieve more productive communications. Use this process flexibly, taking into consideration with whom you are speaking and the business environment (time, stress, needs). By asking the right questions, you can come up with the right strategy. Remember, successful influencers are open to others' ideas and suggestions and focus on mutual understanding.

RESOURCES

Gatto, R. (1990). *A practical guide to effective presentation.* Pittsburgh, PA: GTA Press.

Gibson, J., Ivancevich, J., & Donnelly, J. (1997). *Organizations: Behavior, structure, processes.* Boston, MA: Irwin/McGraw-Hill.

Greenberg, J. (1999). *Managing behavior in organizations* (2nd ed.). Upper Saddle River, NJ: Prentice Hall.

Hiam, A. (1990) *The vest-pocket CEO.* Upper Saddle River, NJ: Prentice Hall.

 # Consultants

How Can I Best Utilize Consultants?

To consult: To give advice or information; to exchange views; to confer; to advise, counsel, and mentor.

HIRING A CONSULTANT takes a lot of skill, more skill than many people realize. The information contained in this chapter will help you know which questions to ask in order to hire the best consultant for your specific purposes.

There are two types of consultants, internal and external. *Internal consultants* are employees who belong to an organization and work to develop that organization. Often the strength and main selling point for using internal consultants is their understanding of the organizational culture, that is, the internal workings and development of long-term relationships with other employees. However, internal consultants are limited in their influence by internal political pressure.

External consultants can guide and advise an organization, but are not affiliated with it. This can be a strength as well as a weakness. As disinterested third parties, they can avoid being drawn into internal organizational issues, but they may be less effective if they are ignorant of those issues.

Both internal and external consultants focus on organizational outcomes. Although there are pros and cons to using either one, the question is which is more appropriate for the situation and why. Because both are assumed to possess a similar skill base, there is very little difference between internal and external consultants with regard to what they can do for you. Both want to influence and change the organization by affecting performance.

External consultants are sometimes hired to be fired, that is, to deliver bad news to top executives. They can sit with people in upper management, with whom they have no history nor expect a future with, and explain the problems in the organization; they don't have to worry about retribution or damage to their consulting careers. In contrast, internal consultants know the company, nuances about the organizational culture, and the employees themselves. Internal consultants may need to worry about giving feedback to top executives, who are known to "shoot the messenger."

Both external and internal consultants have a place in an organization. To choose one over the other, think of the end results and the process needed to achieve those results.

Effective Consultants

The effective consultant formulates questions, listens and acquires clarity about consulting goals, sets a plan, develops a process, and gets buy-in and involvement from the client(s). The following is a list of attributes that you should look for in a consultant:

- Consults without trying to please the client; focuses on critical facts. The consultant may have to say that the client is the problem, something most clients do not want to hear.
- Guides the client to take action.
- Confronts issues and people to make a difference.

- Is able to identify what is occurring.
- Is able to identify, honestly and confidently, goals, obstacles, actions, and follow-through to achieve the consulting goals.
- Has a sense of organizational empowerment and self-empowerment to take action and advise.
- Is able to communicate in a way that influences clients' decisions, not because of position power, but because of data, rapport, and communication style.
- Demonstrates courage of conviction.
- Confronts difficult issues.
- Takes risks.
- Builds a partnership with clients.
- Demonstrates own beliefs.
- Is flexible.
- Does not assume a role or organizational level of authority.

Questions to Discuss

In addition to the above, make sure that you and the consultant consider the following seven questions:

1. What are the organization's goals?
2. What are the organization's strengths?
3. What are the organization's problems?
4. Where could future problems arise?
5. Why do you feel the need to hire a consultant?
6. What needs to be eliminated from the organization?
7. What results are you looking for from the consulting intervention?

A consultant needs the answers to the above questions at a minimum to even begin to understand your corporate culture before conferring, advising, counseling, or mentoring you and your employees.

Organizational Surveys

The following organizational survey is a sample of how a consultant can collect information. The purpose of an organizational survey like this one is to assess employees' attitudes and perceptions. A consultant may need this information to better advise managers on next steps. When hiring a consultant, ask for a sample of the survey that the consultant intends to use. Compare it with this one. The consultant's survey should contain the items below.

Sample Organizational Survey

Instructions: Respond to each item on the survey using the following scale to indicate your level of agreement with the statement:

	High				Low
1. Employees are motivated to perform their jobs effectively.	5	4	3	2	1
2. Employees openly communicate their ideas.	5	4	3	2	1
3. Employees receive recognition for outstanding work.	5	4	3	2	1
4. Employees have a high level of morale.	5	4	3	2	1
5. Employees are kept appropriately informed about business issues and changes.	5	4	3	2	1
6. Employees understand and implement the business goals and objectives of the organization.	5	4	3	2	1
7. Employees are valued and respected.	5	4	3	2	1
8. Employees' ideas are appropriately listened to and acknowledged.	5	4	3	2	1
9. Management supports what it says with action.	5	4	3	2	1

	High	Low

10. Management takes appropriate and decisive action.   5 4 3 2 1

11. Your own work objectives are clear.   5 4 3 2 1

12. Management's leadership style is appropriate for you.   5 4 3 2 1

13. There are appropriate, visible signs throughout the organization showing progress and achievement.   5 4 3 2 1

14. The level of trust among employees is   5 4 3 2 1

15. Employee input is valued.   5 4 3 2 1

16. Employees have a commitment to work together.   5 4 3 2 1

17. Employees are encouraged to express their individual perspectives and ideas.   5 4 3 2 1

18. All employees exhibit a team approach to work issues.   5 4 3 2 1

19. Employees are praised effectively and appropriately.   5 4 3 2 1

20. Employee benefits are fair, equitable, and appropriate.   5 4 3 2 1

21. Employee compensation (pay) is fair, equitable, and appropriate.   5 4 3 2 1

22. Expectations management has of your job are realistic.   5 4 3 2 1

23. The work ethic held by a majority of employees promotes a productive work environment.   5 4 3 2 1

24. There is a cooperative atmosphere of teamwork among employees.   5 4 3 2 1

25. A sense of equity (fairness) exists between management and employees.   5 4 3 2 1

26. The performance appraisal system is fair and equitable.   5 4 3 2 1

	High	Low
27. Customers' needs are appropriately met.	5 4 3 2 1	
28. Employees are given equal opportunity to receive promotions.	5 4 3 2 1	
29. Employees are treated equally and fairly.	5 4 3 2 1	
30. Employees generally feel their work is challenging and rewarding.	5 4 3 2 1	

The survey questions above can be altered as needed, and more can be added. The employees' responses will give the consultant information about strengths and problems within the organization. This information needs to be analyzed by the consultant, interpreted for next-step actions, and presented to the manager.

The Consulting Process

One of the most influential roles of a consultant is being a leader. Setting direction, guiding others, controlling outcomes, and respecting employees show that the consultant can be trusted and is worthy of being heard. It is important that the consultant work with you and other managers in a team approach. An effective consultant, working with the members of the organization, creates expectations, works as a partner, organizes change activities, acts in the interest of both employees and the organization, and provides closure for any activity or change. The main activities of a consultant are described briefly below.

Creates Expectations; Sets Direction

- Helps to write a mission statement, goals, and objectives. Answers the question: What does the organization want to accomplish?
- Identifies the "why's" of the organization, and the "how to's" fall into place.

- Identifies measurable accomplishments and/or results and knows what the organization has done and when.
- Identifies benefits of the outcome.

Works Together; Shares Input

- Sets ground rules as to how you will work together. Creates an effective and efficient manner to establish individual responsibilities. Sets time frames to accomplish the objectives. Gives credit for jobs well done.
- Establishes a way to discuss issues and work through problems.
- Learns to develop alternatives.

Organizes Change Efforts; Sets Priorities

- Has a clearly defined role or responsibility and understands it.
- Encourages managers to utilize their departmental strengths to fulfill their responsibilities.

Acts for Employees and Organization; Takes the Right Action

- Has a voice in the proceeding; his or her input is invaluable.
- Encourages managers to share what they feel safe and comfortable in sharing.
- Identifies and supports each manager's actions.
- Develops a plan of action and implements it.

Provides Closure; Summarizes

- Develops an open, honest, trusting, and respectful relationship with organization members.
- Focuses on what has been accomplished; recognizes achievement.
- Identifies follow-up action: What still needs to be accomplished?
- Summarizes benefits, what people will be or are doing differently because of the consulting intervention.

RESOURCES

Argyris, C. (2000). *Flawed advice and the management trap*. London, England: Oxford University Press.

Block, P. (2000). *Flawless consulting* (2nd ed.). San Francisco, CA: Jossey-Bass/Pfeiffer.

Boyett, J., & Boyett, J. (1998). *The guru guide*. New York: Wiley.

Gatto, R. (1992). *Teamwork through flexible leadership*. Pittsburgh, PA: GTA Press.

Gibson, J., Ivancevich, J., & Donnelly, J. (1997). *Organizations: Behavior, structure, processes*. Boston, MA: Irwin/McGraw-Hill.

Hiam, A. (1990). *The vest-pocket CEO*. Upper Saddle River, NJ: Prentice Hall.

Customers

What Are the Keys to Working with Customers?

A SIX-POINT PLAN for a commonsense approach to working with customers is described in this chapter. You may already be doing some of these things, but look at this list from your customers' point of view to make sure you are doing all you can to maximize the benefits of your customer relationships.

1. Identify What You Want to Accomplish

- What are the end results you want? Guide the customers to clarify expectations. What are they thinking? How will they evaluate results?

- What will cause you to achieve what you want? What product or service will you provide? What customer interaction and rapport will you need to build?

- What are the possible outcomes? Discuss alternatives/ what will occur. Discuss a step-by-step approach.

- Think about the best/worst scenarios. Discuss possible problems (worst case). Discuss what happens when everything falls into place (best case).

- Often customers are not sure what they want. It is your job to help clarify and guide customers to a better understanding of the service/products they need from you.

2. Be Responsible for Achieving What You Want

- Take action. Work independently and have the self-confidence to act.

- Adapt your style of interaction to match that of the customer. Reflect and use your personality and communication skills, learning and working styles.

- Initiate the action that aligns with customer expectations and that you feel will make you successful while meeting customer needs.

- Lay out a plan for achieving the customer's goal. Be assertive by initiating action, demonstrating your commitment, and following through to meet customer expectations.

- Use the computer to establish a strong link between customer needs and your company's services. Digital information and data storage are great aids in providing service.

3. Establish a Focused Direction Along with Priorities

- Customers need to know your thinking about how you will provide product and/or service. Discuss how you envision what will happen.

- Make sure the customer's priorities are your priorities.

4. Develop Alternative Solutions to Come to Agreement

- Let the customers know that you have a flexible approach to meeting their needs.

- While you provide a flexible approach, focus on the customers' stated needs.

- Preventing conflict between people is very important; agreement needs to be discussed and established, rather than taken for granted or assumed.

- Negotiate in a collaborative manner to establish expectations. Negotiations have to be focused and honest.

5. Communicate by Creating a Mutual Understanding

- Clearly identify the topic to be discussed.
- Ask the customer to express his or her needs.
- Be quiet and listen and learn what the customer needs; then express your thoughts, bridging the customer's needs and what you can offer.
- Be sure you and the customer agree on specific issues, such as money, delivery dates, and schedules.
- Be sure to ask the hard questions. Don't avoid raising problems. Do not leave saying, "I should have asked, but I know he/she was upset so I could not bring it up." Alleviating discomfort is only a short-term benefit.
- Establish trust. Be open, respectful, and willing to listen.
- Do not go in knowing the answers. The best way to build rapport with people is to listen to them.

6. Cooperate

- Two minds are better than one. Share your ideas and get the customer involved.
- The more you and the customer work together, the better the working relationship and the outcome. If you and the customer discuss issues, a sharing will occur and less finger pointing will take place if a problem arises.
- Build a collaborative relationship with your customer.

By using these six points, you should be able to satisfy both your company's needs and also those of your customers.

RESOURCES

Albrecht, K., & Zemke, R. (1985). *Service America*. New York: Dow Jones-Irwin.

Covey, S. (1989). *The seven habits of highly effective people*. New York: Simon and Schuster.

Gates, B. (1999). *Business at the speed of thought.* New York: Time Warner.

Willingham, R. (1987). *Integrity selling.* New York: Doubleday.

Yeomans, W. (1985).*1000 things you never learned in business school.* New York: McGraw-Hill.

How Can I Use a Customer Profile to Serve My Customers in Better Ways?

A CUSTOMER PROFILE helps you to learn more about your customers. The purpose is to identify characteristics of your customers in order to understand and serve them better. By using the questions on the following profile, you can "profile" your customers. When you have a customer's profile, you will be able to develop a customized strategy for dealing with that customer.

By completing Part 1 of the profile below, you will determine your customer's preference for either a fact-oriented or a people-oriented interaction. Then, in Part 2, you will answer a series of questions about your customer and devise a plan for working with him or her in the best way possible.

Part 1: Customer Profile

Instructions: Select one of your customers and write his or her name below where indicated. If you want to profile several customers, make copies of the profile for each one. Take a few minutes to reflect on this customer's characteristics and rate your customer on each item in the inventory, using the scale from 1 (never) to 5 (almost always). For this profile to be useful, you must respond honestly. Circle the appropriate number for each question.

5	4	3	2	1
Almost Always	Frequently	Sometimes	Rarely	Never

Name of Customer: _____

This customer is:

1. Quiet; does not express his or her thoughts.   5 4 3 2 1

2. Outgoing, openly expresses his or her thoughts.   5 4 3 2 1

3. Focused primarily on getting the job done.   5 4 3 2 1

4. An effective problem solver.   5 4 3 2 1

5. Analytical and logical.   5 4 3 2 1

6. Concerned with the big picture.   5 4 3 2 1

7. Set in a routine or schedule.   5 4 3 2 1

8. Quick to draw conclusions.   5 4 3 2 1

9. Concerned about building rapport with people.   5 4 3 2 1

10. Very imaginative and intuitive.   5 4 3 2 1

11. Friendly and down-to-earth.   5 4 3 2 1

12. A very expressive communicator, often overemphasizing points.   5 4 3 2 1

13. A blunt-spoken, very brief communicator.   5 4 3 2 1

5	4	3	2	1
Almost Always	Frequently	Sometimes	Rarely	Never

14. Detail-oriented and likes to scrutinize all communication.   5 4 3 2 1

15. A sincere, supportive communicator.   5 4 3 2 1

16. Very flexible, for example, a one-hour meeting could take three hours as his/her thoughts jump from one thing to another.   5 4 3 2 1

17. Very structured, that is, point one leads to point two; a one-hour meeting is one hour sharp.   5 4 3 2 1

18. Emotional and often jumps to conclusions.   5 4 3 2 1

19. Unemotional and sticks to the facts.   5 4 3 2 1

20. The type of person who needs a lot of personal attention.   5 4 3 2 1

21. Someone who demands details.   5 4 3 2 1

22. An effective listener.   5 4 3 2 1

23. Someone who establishes priorities.   5 4 3 2 1

24. Someone who knows exactly what he/she wants.   5 4 3 2 1

25. Someone who speaks without preparation and is able to verbalize ideas quickly.   5 4 3 2 1

26. Concerned with facts and figures.   5 4 3 2 1

27. A person who procrastinates.   5 4 3 2 1

28. A person who does what he/she says he/she will do.   5 4 3 2 1

29. An innovator.   5 4 3 2 1

30. Receptive and listens to others.   5 4 3 2 1

Scoring the Customer Profile

Instructions: Refer to the numbers you circled for your customer on the profile above and place the score for each question on the appropriate line below. Then total your answers.

1 _____	2 _____
3 _____	6 _____
4 _____	9 _____
5 _____	10 _____
7 _____	11 _____
8 _____	12 _____
13 _____	15 _____
14 _____	16 _____
17 _____	18 _____
19 _____	20 _____
21 _____	22 _____
23 _____	25 _____
24 _____	27 _____
26 _____	29 _____
28 _____	30 _____

Total: _____ _____

Fact-Oriented
(to the point;
direct)

People Oriented
(willing to listen;
expressive)

Interpreting the Customer Profile

The two possible customer profiles are fact-oriented and people-oriented. If your customer is fact-oriented, he or she likes to exchange statistics and specific facts when interacting with people. If your customer is people-oriented, he or she is more interested in getting to know you as a person, in making sure that you are comfortable, keying in on your feelings, not necessarily on the facts. If you find that your style and the customer's style are the same, it will not be difficult to interact. However, if you are people-oriented and the customer is fact-oriented, make sure that you present specific facts to that customer. Otherwise, your customer may think you are wasting time trying to get to know him or her. Of course, if the customer is people-oriented, you must spend time using your people skills before jumping into the facts.

Compare the ratings you gave this person. Numbers less than 10 points apart, for example, 70 and 65, indicate that the person has a balanced style and is able to deal with you in either mode.

Numbers more than 10 points apart, for example, 45 and 70, mean you'll need to adjust your approach to meet your customer's strongest characteristics or needs. Begin by using the customer's style and work to put your point across. This may take some time. At this point, reflect on your customer's profile and how you might adapt your approach to working with the person.

Working with the Customer

Based on your results from the inventory, briefly write what you need to do to work with this customer effectively.

Part 2: Action Planning

Background Information

A. Identify your customer's major concerns, that is, interaction with people, deadlines, equipment, manufacturing, contracts, negotiations, and so on.

B. What are the customer's service and/or product needs? Record relevant statements that your customer has made.

Results

C. What results do you think your customer wants?

D. What results do you want from this customer?

Based on your answers to Questions A, B, C, and D, write areas of conflict and agreement between you and your customer below.

Areas of Agreement

Areas of Conflict

Customer Strategy Profile

Based on the profile you have created for your customer, develop a business strategy that would help you work effectively with this customer.

How Can I Best Interact with My Customer?

Summary

You have developed a customer profile and plan for dealing with the customer based on that profile. You should now have a better understanding of your customer. Review the information you have written each time you will interact with your customer to update your strategy as necessary to achieve the desired results.

RESOURCES

Bass, B. (1977). *The orientation inventory manual.* Palo Alto, CA: Consulting Psychologists Press.

Bass, B. (1981). *Stogdill's handbook of leadership.* New York: The Free Press.

Gatto, R. *Customer service manual.* Unpublished manuscript. GTA, 733 Washington Road, Pittsburgh, PA 15228.

Glaser, R. (1995). *The interpersonal influence inventory.* King of Prussia, PA: Organization Design and Development.

McCaulley, M.H. (1985). The selection ratio type table: A research strategy for comparing type distributions. *Journal of Psychological Type, 10,* 45–46.

Q How Can I Ensure That My Customers Are Satisfied?

CUSTOMER SATISFACTION is created by identifying and meeting customer needs, wants, and expectations. It is the customer's reaction to and interpretation of the service provided and is the outcome of effective customer service. You can use the following information to ensure the satisfaction of your customers. Satisfied customers are repeat customers.

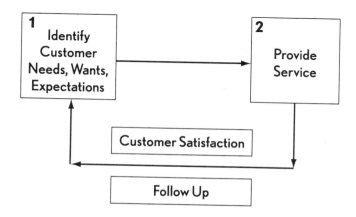

As illustrated in the diagram above, in order to satisfy customers, you first must identify customer needs, wants, and expectations. Customers have the following needs:

- To be listened to and understood;
- To feel appreciated;
- To feel special; and
- To be comfortable.

Customers want or expect service providers:

- To have a positive attitude and outlook;
- To listen first, talk second;
- To show enthusiasm;
- To be flexible and do what it takes to meet reasonable expectations;
- To provide support whether they are right or wrong;
- To provide a personalized approach; and
- To realize that the customer views everything and everyone as part of the organization.

The second step shown on the diagram is to provide appropriate service based on the customer needs. Keep the following list of suggestions in mind as you strive to satisfy your customers:

- Ask questions to identify customer expectations and listen.
- Think about what extra service you can provide internally and externally. Go the extra smile.
- Don't blame others.
- Communicate clearly. Restate and ask questions.
- Take ownership of a customer request. Don't pass it on or say, "I don't handle this." Collect the necessary information and take action.
- Don't share internal information (such as, "Department B is never on time").

- Continue to find ways to enhance the service you provide by continual re-evaluation and investigation of your competition.

- Think ahead—anticipate what will occur. Ask, "What if. . . ?"

As you move to the third step, customer satisfaction, be aware of the following factors that customers consider when assessing service:

Quality

- Were my expectations and needs met?
- Was everything the way it should have been?

Variety

- Were options available from which I could choose?
- What was offered to me?

Personalized Treatment

- Was the staff friendly (greeting customers; answering questions)?
- Were my particular needs and requests met?

Convenience

- Did the organization's personnel make it easy for me to find/do things (return phone calls/give needed directions)?

Timeliness

- Was everything done on time?

Even when you make every attempt to satisfy a customer, sometimes the customer will become hostile. In that case, keep the following suggestions in mind:

- Listen without arguing. Look for agreement.
- Be supportive. Say, "I understand."
- Paraphrase, clarify, and restate the problem.

- Respond with facts and information, not emotions, to resolve the concerns.
- Develop a plan to resolve the problem. The customer is not always right, but that doesn't mean you should tell the customer that he or she is wrong. Instead, using the techniques listed above, you may be able to reach an understanding.

Take a few moments to think about the customer service that your organization provides and make some notes about it below.

What is being done right?

What needs to be improved?

What can you do to enhance customer service?

RESOURCES

Albrecht, K., & Zemke, R. (1985). *Service America!* Homewood, IL: Dow Jones-Irwin.

Gatto, R. *Customer service manual.* Unpublished manuscript. GTA, 733 Washington Road, Pittsburgh, PA 15228.

 **Interviewing**

What Kinds of Questions Should I Ask When Conducting an Interview?

INTERVIEWING IS THE ART of asking the right questions and listening carefully to what the interviewee says as well as to what the interviewee doesn't say. Keep the following advice in mind when preparing to interview a job candidate.

- Ask questions that focus on background, up-to-date technical and general knowledge, and people skills relevant to the position.

- Ask open-ended questions to create a dialogue.

- Set a relaxed, businesslike climate. The atmosphere you build sets the stage for an exchange of ideas. Don't come across as though you have better things to do or have been interviewing all day.

- Begin by explaining the purpose of the interview, what you hope to accomplish.

- Prepare for an interview carefully, so as not to bias yourself by collecting too much information, by comparing the candidate immediately to other candidates, or by allowing personal prejudice. Establish a fair mind-set prior to the interview.

- Remember to listen carefully and to take good notes.

Types of Interview

Decide which of the following types of interview you will be doing.

- *Unstructured Interview:* Format and questions are left to the discretion of the interviewer.
- *Structured Interview:* Use of a predetermined list of questions to which all interviewees are asked to respond (usually in a written format). These questions can be sent out to all the candidates ahead of time and then used as a basis for comparison when they are returned.
- *Situational Interview:* Focus is on the behaviors needed to be successful on the job. For example, you might ask a candidate to describe his or her style of communication if the job will require the person to interact with people on a regular basis.

Questions

The following list contains some good questions that can help elicit the information necessary to be able to evaluate a job candidate.

- Give an overview of your experience.
- What are you hoping to achieve by moving to a new position?
- How have your work experiences prepared you for this position?
- Describe your current/previous job. What were your successes? What were your areas for improvement?
- Describe your previous supervisor or manager. In what ways were you alike? In what ways were you different?

- Describe an unpleasant or stressful on-the-job experience. How did you handle it?
- Describe challenges from your current/previous jobs. How did you meet those challenges?
- Was planning an important aspect of your previous job? When and how do you do planning?
- Describe your decision-making style. (For example, do you consult co-workers, read relevant material, ask the boss, do it on your own?)
- Describe your method of communication with other employees.
- Describe your style of leadership.
- What were the significant learning experiences in your life so far?
- Describe the conditions in which you work best.
- On what developmental plans are you presently working?

In addition, ask specific questions about the technical aspects of the job.

Listen carefully to what the candidate says for indications of any of these issues:

- Problem-Solving Ability
- Leadership Ability
- Positive Attitude
- Ability to Collaborate
- Concern for Others
- Style of Communication
- Sincerity
- Listening
- Poor Eye Contact
- Organizational Skills

- Problems with Authority
- Negative Feelings
- Control
- Self-Orientation
- Disinterest
- Immaturity
- Interruptions
- Nervousness
- Disorganization
- Complaining

Checking References

After the interview, it is a good idea to check three or four of the references provided to ensure that the information the candidate provided is factual. The following are some questions to ask the person used as a reference:

- What were the candidate's responsibilities on his or her last job?
- Did the candidate fulfill the responsibilities?
- What is the candidate's work ethic?
- How does the candidate work under pressure?
- How does the candidate interact with co-workers and/or with superiors?
- Is there anything in particular that stands out about this candidate?
- Why would you hire this person?
- How does this person communicate ideas?
- If this person were in a meeting, would he/she make a difference?

By obtaining a composite picture from several references, in addition to verifying what the candidate told you, you can avoid a personality clash. If, for example, one reference states that the candidate was difficult to work with, but three state that this person was a wonderful team player, you might assume the problem is with the one reference, and not with the candidate.

Two Interview Examples

The following are examples of two different job interviews. They are written questions and the interviewees' written answers. The first person has applied for a plant manager position and the second for an accountant's position.

1. In general, describe your plant background.

   Twenty-three years' experience as operations engineer and plant manager, working in design, plant start-ups, and quality management.

2. Describe your ability and skills as a supervisor.

   I communicate well, understand how to refine processes, and have strong ability to instruct and teach others.

3. Discuss your style of working and leadership style with others.

   I like to have people who clearly understand what is expected and let them know that they are accountable.

4. What is your method to evaluate performance?

   Goals and objectives are outlined, and performance objectives are measurable and clearly understood by both the supervisor and the employee.

5. How will you resolve problems and issues that will confront you daily?

   Collect the data/information and evaluate these data against the issue or problem. Collect facts and evaluate.

6. What do you feel would be the main pressures in a plant manager position?

   Personnel issues not related to the normal work routine.

7. What strategy or method do you use to address work-related pressures?

   Collect and evaluate information and anticipate the unexpected.

8. Describe the type of supervisory skills you have acquired over your career.

   People like to be treated fairly (not always equal, but fair). Communication is critical to a successful operation. Teach people to do their job and hold them accountable.

9. Describe why you are an effective plant manager.

   I train people well and let them know what is expected of them.

10. What suggestions did you make at your last position?

    Using stamp changing and real blend variation.

11. Describe your organizational skills.

    I believe in planning and following a plan.

12. What is the main reason for leaving your present or last position?

    Health reasons and disagreement with the boss.

13. What experience do you feel you have gained from previous positions that would benefit you in a plant manager position?

    People are key to an organization, and employees can make the difference between success and failure.

14. Describe an unpleasant or stressful on-the-job situation in a prior position and how you handled it.

    I was forced to fire an employee for fighting in the plant.

15. What are you hoping to accomplish by taking this new position?

    I am interested in a career as a plant manager to apply the skills I have refined for the past twenty-three years.

Note that this person's responses are brief, direct, and very businesslike. No personal experiences are given. This interviewee did not share his feelings or thoughts outside the scope of the question.

This type of written interview can be very useful in comparing candidate responses. After reviewing the answers to all the written questions briefly, an interviewer can then conduct a situational and/or unstructured interview in person with the final candidates. Here's another example.

1. In general, describe your accounting background.

    I began in 1974 in cost accounting; I have a very strong cost-accounting background in manufacturing. I have done cost-analyst studies on warehousing. I did cost analysis at Titanium Metals, including payables, receivables, warehouse inventory, and credit checks. I have done budgeting and forecasting. I have used all types of financial statements. I have done audits each year.

2. Describe your ability and skills as an accountant.

I have done payables, receivables, cost analysis, warehouse inventory, operational audits, payroll, feasibility studies, and financial packages for banks. I have worked as a budget manager and with CPA firms doing audits.

3. Discuss your style of working with others.

I am flexible. I like to get to know people, interacting with them and treating them as individuals. As a leader, I focus on teamwork.

4. What is your method to evaluate and implement accounting procedures?

I view the business like an outside auditor. I believe that every company is different and that it is important to know the company's products and services. I meet with management, establish a plan, implement it, and get feedback to meet schedules. I've done audits to implement accounting procedures.

5. How will you resolve accounting problems and issues that will confront you daily?

I use the following steps: (a) understand what the problem is, (b) identify the cause of the problem, (c) assess immediate need, (d) prioritize the various problems and bring in appropriate people who can solve them, (e) get the facts, (f) be aware of all information collected to assess the problem, (g) solve the problem and make sure it is solved.

6. What do you feel would be the main pressures in an accounting position such as this?

The two main pressures would be (1) deadlines and (2) that anything can happen, even if you plan well.

7. What strategy/method do you use to address work-related pressures?

I would make sure I have a thorough knowledge of the company. I would also hold weekly meetings to increase my awareness of what is happening on a day-to-day basis.

8. Describe why you are an effective accountant.

   I am creative. I like business leadership. I have three areas of strength: computers, science, and mathematics; I like all three of these aspects. Being a successful accountant is putting together what I like: working in computer programming, science, and math.

9. What accounting suggestions did you make at your last position?

   I was involved in budgeting. I put in financial controls. I developed a model that forecast financial success, for example, cash flow, income, and balance sheet by monthly estimating. I showed how to use this in quarterly meetings and tax planning.

10. Describe your organizational skills.

    I consider myself to be very organized, which helps me to solve problems. If I don't know something, I learn where the information is. I keep logs of all my activities, from computer use to accounting.

11. Describe your experience in preparing quarterly compilations or reviews.

    At my previous company, I did all financials for each quarter. I also did all the analysis and graphics.

12. Describe the day-to-day duties you performed in your last job as an accountant.

    I managed budgeting, financial modeling, and payroll. I monitored where everything was and ensured accuracy. I made sure all of the information was organized. I did feasibility studies. I know communication is critical; I kept people informed.

13. Describe your style of communicating.

    I want to know more about what you think; then I talk. I like to listen. I like to discuss issues; I use a team approach that encourages open two-way discussion.

14. If there is an accounting problem with a statement, how would you resolve it?

   First, I would find out whether it is an error. Then I would identify what caused the problem. Next, I would let upper management know about the problem and I would explain it. Finally, I would generate a plan and go and fix the problem.

15. What is (are) the main reason(s) for leaving your present or last position?

   Middle-management layoff.

16. What experiences do you feel you have gained from previous positions that would benefit you in an accountant's position?

   I have experience with a wide variety of products and services. I have interfaced with all departments, getting to know the whole company. I have worked with all levels of employees, from the president to secretaries.

17. Describe the best use of your business-related talents.

   I know PC computers and have a certificate in computer programming. I use all of these skills in accounting. I have also conducted all types of accounting feasibility studies.

18. Describe an unpleasant or stressful on-the-job situation in a prior position and how you handled it.

   At a previous company, I worked with a metallurgist who was very aggressive. I remained calm; listened to him; worked with him; built a relationship with him; gave him useful information. We ended up having a very good working relationship.

19. What are you hoping to accomplish by taking this new position?

   I want to do a good job and help the company fulfill this job so I can fulfill my life and family needs.

20. Comment about yourself.

I am dedicated. I arrive early to work and will work late and on weekends as necessary. I maintain a solid reputation. I enjoy what I am doing. I have a lot of experience fixing financial problems.

Following is a comparison of the responses of the two candidates. Keep in mind that they were applying for two different positions and, therefore, the questions varied slightly.

Area of Comparison	Interviewee 1	Interviewee 2
Communication Style	Brief and succinct	Expressive and detailed
Skills	Focused— singled out a key skill	Big picture— identified multiple skills
Thinking	Sequential information	General information
Needs (in an interview)	This person has to be drawn out	This person may need to be refocused
Focus	Focused on factual representation	Focused on general background information

If you, as a manager, have a bias toward or against either of these two styles (specific versus global) you must recognize that bias. Your job is to find the best-qualified person for the job, the one who can best perform the required tasks and responsibilities. Your approach to finding the best candidate should focus on the job requirements, environment, fellow employees, customers, product, service, and management expectations. For example, if you need someone who can handle multiple tasks and deal with the public, you may tailor what you are looking for toward the characteristics of someone like Interviewee 2. However, if you want someone who is highly task-oriented, you may want to look at someone like Interviewee 1. Both of these candidates, although different in work habits and style, were hired and are successful in their different positions.

RESOURCES

Bell, A.H. (1989). *The complete manager's guide to interviewing.* Homewood, IL: Dow Jones-Irwin.

Fear, R., & Chiron, R.J. (1990). *The evaluation interview.* New York: McGraw-Hill.

Gatto, R. (1991). *A practical guide to effective presentation.* Pittsburgh, PA: GTA Press.

Gatto, R. (1990). *Characteristic profile.* Pittsburgh, PA: GTA Press.

Hiam, A. (1990). *The vest pocket CEO.* Upper Saddle River, NJ: Prentice Hall.

Personnel Policy Services, Inc. (2000). Application and interview questions. *Personnel policy manual.* Louisville, KY: Author.

Schultz, D., & Schultz, S. (1998). *Psychology and work today.* Upper Saddle River, NJ: Prentice Hall.

Q How Can I Prepare to Be Interviewed?

WHEN THE TABLES ARE TURNED and you are being interviewed, prepare to answer all types of questions. By preparing, you will not be caught off guard and will have already thought of the ideas and experiences to show yourself in the best light.

First, you must investigate the company you are interviewing with. Here's how.

- Go to the library to find background information on the company.

- Visit the company's headquarters, stores, or plants to see work in action.

- Use the Internet to find up-to-date information.

- Speak with business acquaintances and ask their opinions about the company.

Second, use the following questions to prepare for an interview:

1. Based on your understanding, describe the position's responsibilities.

2. What skills and abilities do you have that will fulfill the responsibilities of the position, and is there an opportunity for advancement?

3. Briefly describe your work ethic.

4. What method do you use to evaluate and implement ideas and business decisions?

5. How will you resolve problems and issues that will confront you daily?

6. What do you think would be the main pressures in a position such as this?

7. What strategy/method do you use to address pressures in your life?

8. How would you build a team with other professionals in an organization?

9. Describe why you are an effective decision maker.

10. Describe the opportunities this company would offer you to grow.

11. How do you give presentations?

12. How is this business cyclical in nature?

13. Describe your style of leadership. Why are you an effective leader?

14. Describe how you could be an advisor to your boss.

15. What did you implement or suggest in your last position to improve the growth of business or productivity?

16. What is (are) the main reason(s) for leaving your present or last position?

17. What knowledge have you gained from previous positions that would benefit you in this position?

18. Describe the best use of your business-related talents.

19. Describe an unpleasant or stressful on-the-job situation and how you handled it.

20. What are you hoping to accomplish by taking this new position?

21. What are the overriding thoughts you have about yourself and having a job?

Third, in addition to researching the company and preparing for the interview, remember the following:

- What you don't say is important. You do not want to ramble and thus appear disorganized, but at the same time, you may not want to be too brief in your answers, perhaps indicating an unwillingness to share information.

- Be yourself, relax, and don't put undue pressure on yourself. Keep in mind that everyone—including your interviewer—has been in the interviewee seat.

- Be aware of your own nonverbals. Don't sit in a slouchy manner, nor do you want your posture to appear too rigid. Make sure that you make eye contact with the interviewer, but not to the point of staring.

By being aware of the above points, investigating the company ahead of time, and preparing for the interview itself, you give yourself the best chance to make a positive impression during an interview.

RESOURCES

Bell, A.H. (1989). *The complete manager's guide to interviewing.* Homewood, IL: Dow Jones-Irwin.

Fear, R., & Chiron, R.J. (1990). *The evaluation interview.* New York: McGraw-Hill.

Gatto, R. (1991). *A practical guide to effective presentation.* Pittsburgh, PA: GTA Press.

Gatto, R. (2000). *Characteristics profile.* Pittsburgh, PA: GTA Press.

Personnel Policy Services, Inc. (2000). Application and interview questions. *Personnel policy manual.* Louisville, KY: Author.

Schultz, D., & Schultz, S. (1998). *Psychology and work today.* Upper Saddle River, NJ: Prentice Hall.

 **Leadership**

QWhat Are the Qualities of an Effective Leader?

LEADERSHIP OCCURS when people guide and develop themselves and others by communicating direction, taking appropriate action, building trust, and achieving goals within a changing environment (Gatto, 1992).

Leadership skills are observable, constant, and stable. However, each person's skill as a leader varies because of opportunity, stress, frustration, employee abilities, individual desires, and time limitations. Because all these factors may affect your ability to lead, be aware of how these pressures impact your leadership skills. For example, if a position requires seventy hours a week to be effective, and you choose to spend more time with your family and fifty hours a week at work, your ability to lead may be compromised. As a leader matures and takes on more responsibility, he or she is required to demonstrate greater ability, such as the ability to interact with others or store, synthesize, and retrieve information. Additionally, an experienced leader is expected to have the self-confidence and self-esteem to interact in a changing workplace, making choices that affect the entire organization.

Effective leaders use various leadership styles. Your abilities and skills—and those of the people you lead—in a situation determine the appropriate leadership style you should use. Leaders trust themselves to act in unpredictable situations and develop skills while leading and developing others. Effective leaders know when and to whom to listen and follow. They know how to apply their abilities to the opportunity.

There is no one right way to lead effectively; however, a leader must consider the following:

- His/her abilities and skills as a leader.
- The maturity, know-how, and knowledge of the people the leader is leading.
- What constitutes an appropriate action or response in a given circumstance, changing situation, or environment.
- Business or corporate expectations.
- The personal desire to achieve and to act decisively.

Effective Leaders

1. Clearly define goals, direction, and responsibilities for each working associate.

2. Successfully communicate necessary information to all associates on an equal basis.

3. Work with associates to establish expected results and achieve those results.

4. Reassess expected results and methods of action by providing updates to associates.

5. Use the right person for the specific job function.

6. Ensure that associates perform necessary tasks and give them credit for their achievements.

7. Reassess daily business needs in relationship to available staff.

8. Give capable associates the freedom to meet job expectations via their individual styles of working.

9. Build an open, trusting, respectful, and honest rapport with all working associates.

10. Give working associates recognition whenever it is deserved.

Leadership Dimensions

You can use the following list as a benchmark for your ability to lead. Think of a leader whom you admire. Think about which of the leadership dimensions listed the person demonstrates. If this person is an effective leader, he or she would have demonstrated each of these dimensions. You can also look at yourself to see what dimensions you need to enhance to achieve the level of a leader.

Leader   Yourself

——— ——— Demonstrate competence, confidence, and caring for associates.

——— ——— Translate goals, direction, and vision into customer satisfaction.

——— ——— Involve followers; listen to their points of view and suggestions; share information; be willing to be influenced.

——— ——— Be flexible to changing business and associates' needs and demands; be innovative.

——— ——— Create a safe environment that encourages the development of associates so they can become future leaders.

——— ——— Identify strengths and opportunities for development for oneself and others.

——— ——— Continually reassess goals, direction, and vision to meet customer needs; support innovation.

——— ——— Think of serving associates through leadership; make a contribution that is lasting; transform the present into the desired future.

——— ——— Build trust through actions that equal words; set an appropriate example.

Leadership Styles

The following grid illustrates four general styles of leadership; no one style is best. The most appropriate style of leadership depends on the situation and the abilities of the leader and associate(s). Therefore, effective leaders need to be flexible. Think of leadership as a tight/loose relationship—"tight" means setting the parameters, policy procedures, and responsibilities, then turning the associates "loose" to accomplish their responsibilities.

The traditional way of looking at leadership style is based on the leader exhibiting certain behaviors given the situation. In other words, it is the behaviors that determine the relationship with the followers.

Leadership Styles Grid

	Participative ❸ (TO) Low (PO) High	Share/Consult ❷ (TO) High (PO) High
	Empower/ Delegate ❹ (TO) Low (PO) Low	Direct ❶ (TO) High (PO) Low

High ←→ Low (Leader's Involvement, People Oriented)

Low —— Leader's Control —— High

Task Oriented

PO = People-oriented
TO = Task-oriented
(Gatto, 1991)

There are many leadership models, such as Trait Theory (Stogdill, 1974) that identify specific characteristics within a leader, or the Situational Leadership theory (Blanchard, Zigarmi, & Zigarmi, 1985) that advocates that a leader understand his or her behaviors and the behaviors of followers within a given situation. An explanation of a general leadership model, shown above, follows.

Direct

This authoritarian (or directing) leadership style is high in control, with results a priority. This leader closely supervises the decision-making process. Such task-oriented leaders expect associates to get the job done.

This style is used appropriately with new associates or associates who lack knowledge, skill, or ability. This leader initiates, organizes, and directs associates to accomplish a task. When interaction or communication is limited, this style also may be appropriate. Many leaders fall into the "I can do the job better than the associate" trap; therefore the leader does the job.

Associates generally don't develop leadership skills under this style because they do not learn how to accomplish a task on their own. They also do not receive recognition for the completed job. The leader using this style should continually reassess associates' abilities. When an associate has the expertise to achieve, and there is sufficient time, another style of leadership may be appropriate.

Share/Consult

This style of leadership builds on the direct style but with a higher degree of interaction between the leader and associates. There is now an exchange of ideas about what needs to be accomplished. The leader, who can be task-oriented as well as people-oriented, can act as an advisor. The leader coaches, motivates, and advises associates.

This style is appropriate when there is sufficient time to interact with and develop associates' abilities. However, the leader still controls because associates may still need to develop more confidence and/or competence. This style begins with sharing ideas with associates about the task. *Caution:* If the leader doesn't implement ideas he or she solicited from associates, morale might suffer. Associates might have expectations that the leader will act on their ideas. For that reason, it is important that the leader set ground rules for expected results. The leader needs to make clear the purpose and reason for sharing information, taking care not to dominate the process. The leader has to integrate what the follower says, summarize agreement, and clarify any conflicts.

Participative

This style, which builds on the sharing style, encourages the development of a trusting relationship between leader and associates. The leader shows trust in associates' ability to complete job responsibilities. The leader builds a mutually respectful relationship by sharing as much information as possible with associates in open, free-flowing discussions. The leader listens, accepts, and cooperates with associates and encourages their participation in the decision-making process.

This style is appropriate when tasks require a lot of interaction between leader and associates (who are also more confident and knowledgeable than at other levels). The participative style is viewed as an effective approach to leadership.

This style is effective because it encourages leaders and competent associates to develop their interaction skills. It also lets associates begin to emerge as leaders by letting them complete a job with less control from the leader. It also opens lines of communication so associates can express their viewpoints and be used as resources. It promotes sharing because associates know their input will be accepted and used. It is important that the leader inform the associates about decisions because not being informed could hinder participation. The participative style helps the leader share and collect information while helping associates become involved in making decisions. The leader must be an effective listener and willing to initiate action based on the participative process.

Empower/Delegate

This style builds on the participative style and lets the follower initiate action.

This style is appropriate when associates are highly confident and competent or when they need little encouragement to accomplish job responsibilities. There is less interaction and control by the leader because now associates emerge as leaders. The leader and the associates should have developed an effective working rapport and should have established mutual trust. The leader can step away from the job and associates without concern that the job will be successfully accomplished. The leader entrusts associates to do the right things, yet still measures the progress from a distance. However, associates can, and are, permitted to make necessary decisions to complete the job. This lets the associates use and develop their skills as leaders.

This leadership style can be a developmental process for both associates and leader, as well as a test for a leadership succession plan in developing future leaders.

Summary

To lead effectively, the leader must choose a style that best fits his or her abilities and considers both the associates' abilities and the changing work environment. It is essential that leaders demonstrate qualities of communication, trust, competence, and confidence in establishing a business direction.

RESOURCES

Bass, B. (1981). *Stogdill's handbook of leadership*. New York: Free Press.

Bennis, W. (1999). *Old dogs, new tricks*. Provo, UT: Executive Excellence Publishing.

Blanchard, K., Zigarmi, K., & Zigarmi, D. (1985). *Leadership and the one-minute manager*. New York: William Morrow.

Covey, S., Jones, D., & Merrill, R. (1999). *The nature of leadership*. Salt Lake City, UT: Franklin Covey.

Drucker, P. (1999). *Management challenges for the 21st century*. New York: HarperCollins.

Fitzgerald, C., & Kirby, L.K. (1997). *Developing leaders: Research and applications in psychological type and leadership development*. Palo Alto, CA: Davies-Black.

Fleishman, E.A. (1973). Twenty years of consideration and structure. In E.A. Fleishman & J.C. Hunt (Eds.), *Current developments in the study of leadership*. Carbondale, IL: Southern Illinois University Press.

Gatto, R. (1992). *Teamwork through flexible leadership*. Pittsburgh, PA: GTA Press.

Gibson, J., Ivancevich, J., & Donnelly, J. (1997). *Organizations: Behavior, structure, processes*. Boston, MA: Irwin/McGraw-Hill.

Schutz, W. (1994). *The human element*. San Francisco, CA: Jossey-Bass.

Meetings

How Can I Make My Meetings More Effective?

MEETINGS CAN BE LIKE money deposited in a bank: when people attend a meeting, they are putting part of their salary in a bank—the meeting! If you have an effective meeting, you receive not only principal but interest on your money. If you conduct an ineffective meeting—one without purpose and measurable results—you are losing principal and interest. For a meeting to be effective, it requires *planning*, an *introduction, interaction,* and a *summary,* as shown in the following chart.

Planning	Introduction	Interaction	Summary
Create focus, don't waste time	What is going to occur; be flexible	Achieve what you want to accomplish	Review information and answer questions
Identify the purpose of the meeting	Introduce topic(s) and speakers	Present topics and/or speakers and clarify needs	State, "In summary" or "In conclusion"
Identify the type of meeting: presenting or collecting information, problem solving, or combination	Explain the meeting's purpose and expected results	Present and bridge your information (facts) and needs to accomplish meeting purpose	Restate important points; paraphrase
	Set ground rules (time frame, asking questions, handouts)		Identify areas of agreement and possible problems
Identify what you want to accomplish and identify measurable results	Review benefits of the meeting	Ask questions; listen and collect information and needs	Discuss and agree on follow-up action
Get the right people involved	If appropriate, bridge prior and/or following meetings	Utilize techniques to focus and control the meeting and involve people	Focus on decisions or consensus; ask, "What do we agree on?"
Create and distribute an agenda. (See below for a sample.)	Identify ways of working together; be proactive, supportive,		Ask how people feel about the decisions

Planning	Introduction	Interaction	Summary
	and innovative; get participation and foster an open dialogue	Be flexible—lead, facilitate, and follow	Establish individual responsibilities for action Thank the people involved

Meeting Agenda

The following outline for a meeting agenda will help you to prepare for an effective meeting. Emphasis should be put on the purpose and what is to be accomplished. This agenda can be broken down into three parts: (1) gathering necessary information, (2) preparing the agenda, and (3) taking notes during the meeting.

Information

Name of Meeting: _____

Date: _____

Time Began: _____

Time Concluded: _____

Place: _____

Attendees: _____

_____

Purpose: _____

_____

Expected Results *(What is to be accomplished?)*: _____

_____

Level of Importance: _____

Agenda *(repeat this section if necessary for multiple topics)*

Topic: _____

Time Available to Discuss: _____

Discussion Leader: _____

Decision(s):

Action(s) to Be Taken:

Time Frame to Accomplish:

People Involved (responsibilities):

Notes:

Follow-Up Questions

1. What do we agree on?

2. What is your commitment to the action?

Meeting Guidelines for the Group Process

Agree on how the group wants to work together by establishing working guidelines. Put those ideas on a flip chart and bring them to each meeting. The illustration below is a list of sample guidelines.

Meeting Guidelines
✓ We will work together in a constructive manner.
✓ We will listen to each person.
✓ One person will speak at a time.
✓ We will stay on the topic.
✓ Ask if all views have been heard... include everyone.
✓ Say what you think.
✓ Ask for agreement.
✓ Ask the right questions.
✓ Listen to disagreement openly.
✓ Identify disrupters.

At the end of the meeting, discuss each point briefly to make sure the group is adhering to the guidelines or to determine whether a particular guideline should be added or deleted.

Hints to Improve Meeting Effectiveness

1. Prepare an agenda and distribute it to all attendees prior to the meeting. Make some extra copies and bring them to the meeting.

2. Check all audiovisual equipment before the meeting.

3. On a flip chart, write the purpose of the meeting and what is to be accomplished.

4. Stand when you begin the meeting. For an informal discussion, sit down after you call the meeting to order. Place yourself in a position from which you will be able to see and respond to all participants.

5. Allow top management people to discuss their specific issues first so they can leave early.

6. Anticipate and encourage group interaction. Break a large group into smaller groups of three or four for small-group discussion.

7. As a facilitator, offer to collect the group's ideas for typing and distribution later.

8. Interject when no new viewpoints on a topic are offered. When the same viewpoints are repeated, members become bored.

9. Table an issue that has not been appropriately resolved; set follow-up action for a later meeting.

10. Control the meeting so it stays within the established time constraints. Do not let a disrupter (interrupter) sidetrack the meeting. However, do encourage input and differing points of view.

11. Follow up a brainstorming or problem-solving session by distributing information to all necessary or appropriate associates.

12. Copy suggestions that have been listed on the flip chart for review.

13. Review next-step actions before concluding.

Brief Meetings

Sometimes a brief meeting must be convened to address a specific issue. The following guidelines will help keep these meetings on point.

- Keep it short, from five to fifteen minutes.
- State the meeting's purpose and the results to be accomplished.
- Stay focused: cover only one or two topics.
- Have everyone stand.
- Have eight or fewer people in attendance.
- Solicit needed input only.
- Summarize agreement and actions to be taken, and gain follow-up commitment.

To improve meeting effectiveness, you must plan. In addition, you must explain the meeting's purpose, identify what you want to accomplish, and summarize what has been accomplished. Finally, you should keep all parties informed and updated.

RESOURCES

Doyle, M., & Strauss, D. (1982). *How to make meetings work*. New York: Jove Books.

Gatto, R. (1992). *Teamwork through flexible leadership*. Pittsburgh, PA: GTA Press.

Silberman, M. (1999). *101 ways to make meetings active*. San Francisco, CA: Jossey-Bass/Pfeiffer.

Q When Facilitating a Meeting, How Can I Deal with Problems?

THE FACILITATOR'S ROLE in a meeting is to encourage and balance participation; to guide discussion without dominating; to keep the discussion on track; and to maintain an open and positive environment in which meeting participants will feel safe to contribute ideas and opinions.

Facilitating a discussion is relatively easy once you master some basic techniques. The following chart identifies some common problems in facilitating discussions and suggests techniques that can help resolve them.

Problem	Facilitation Techniques
No one is participating	Ask the group a general question such as: "How does this apply to your job? What do we need to accomplish in this meeting?" Wait at least ten seconds; someone will usually respond. If not, ask another general question or pull in group members by looking at a specific person or calling someone by name. Use a flip chart and large index cards to have participants write out questions and answers.
One person is dominating the discussion.	Ask the group, "Does anyone have a different thought?" Write the comments on a flip chart. If the first speaker continues to talk, say, "Just a minute, Joe; Bill has a comment." Solicit group input.
One person has not participated.	Ask, a particular person, "John, do you have a thought on this? How does this apply in your area?"
Two or more people are speaking simultaneously.	In a professional manner say, "One at a time. Who wants to go first?" Solicit input from both parties. Make eye contact with one person to show that he/she may begin.
The group gets off on a tangent.	Redirect group thinking by saying, "There are a lot of good ideas, but I think we're off the topic." or "Let's focus on . . . ." If you want to revisit some ideas later, write them on a flip chart.
One participant provides long, detailed examples of past experiences.	Let the speaker talk for a while. Then, gently interject, summarize what's been said, and ask a question that relates the example back to the topic.

Problem	Facilitation Techniques
A participant's comments are not clear.	Ask, "Mary, can you say more about that?" or "Ed, let me see if I understand. Are you saying that [paraphrase]?"
One participant continually interrupts and appears hostile toward the content.	If you're seated, stand up and walk a little closer to the person. Interject, paraphrase the speaker's ideas, and relate them to the topic. Ask others for their views. You might say, "Joe, you sound as though you have strong feelings about this." The speaker may say, "Yes, I'm upset because . . . ." Relate back to this topic. You could use a flip chart to highlight points.
A participant asks a question and you need time to think of a response.	Ask a question in return, such as, "Why do you ask that? That's interesting; could you expand on that? What's the impact? How do you think that could be accomplished?" This will provide information and give you time to think of a response.
A participant asks a question for which you don't know the answer.	State that you don't know. Ask others in the room whether they know. (This may not always be appropriate.) Ask meeting participants if they would like you or someone to look into the issue. Let participants know that you will get back to them with the information and when. (Take this last step only if you are prepared to find the necessary information and provide it to the participants.)

Problem	Facilitation Techniques
One participant is critical of another participant's comments.	Interrupt with a comment such as "Mary, you seem to see this differently from Joe . . . . How do you see it?" If important, put ideas on a flip chart. After the description is finished, if appropriate, comment on differences/conflict and note that differing opinions are good because they allow people to see a variety of ideas. The key is to critique ideas, not people.
Two participants are holding a private conversation.	If their conversation is interrupting the meeting, interject gently, "Carol and Ken, do you have a comment from which everyone can benefit?" If it is not interrupting, speak to them on break.

RESOURCES

Brassard, M., & Ritter, D. (1994). *The memory jogger II*. Boston, MA: Goal/GQC.

Champagne, D., & Hogan, R. (1982). *Consultant supervisor theory and skill development*. Pittsburgh, PA: University of Pittsburgh Press.

Gibson, J., Ivancevich, J., & Donnelly, J. (1997). *Organizations: Behavior, structure, processes*. Boston, MA: Irwin/McGraw-Hill.

Haines, S.G. (1995). *Successful strategic planning*. Menlo Park, CA: Crisp.

Ludden, L., & Capozzoli, T. (2000). *Supervisor savvy*. Indianapolis, IN: JIST Works.

Q How Can I Handle Hostile or Disruptive Groups?

THE NEEDS OF A HOSTILE GROUP have to be addressed calmly and with facts. When the group bands together on an issue, listen intently and then respond. Do not fight emotion with emotion—use facts to influence the group's thinking. By diffusing the hostility, it is possible to find a resolution for the problem. Additionally, a hostile person can actually prove useful by bringing up controversial issues or causing the group to think out of the box.

The following steps can help you to control a hostile situation.

1. If you are seated, stand.

2. Make eye contact with all the people in the room.

3. Help the group to participate in the discussion by calling on individuals.

4. Keep pace with the group members by using their style of speech and jargon. Speak on their level.

5. If a hostile person presents facts, copy the facts on paper or a flip chart. This makes the person feel listened to and helps diffuse hostility.

6. Get a clear understanding of the problem. Listen to what is said and address the issue to negotiate a mutually satisfying resolution. Control the discussion by asking the who, what, when, where, and why questions and recording the responses on a flip chart.

7. If you know the answer, state it, giving background and results. If you do not know the answer, tell the group that you don't know, that you will find out as soon as possible, and when you will get the information to them.

8. Do not continue repeating a point; focus on specific facts.

9. Stay with the topic until the level of hostility has been lowered. You may need several meetings to do this.

10. Recap the discussion by verbally addressing the main issues and, if possible, visually highlighting points using a flip chart or overhead.

11. If possible, when you see that no new information is being added, take a short break to relieve tension.

When handling a hostile group in a meeting, it is essential that you remain calm. Ask questions and stay with the facts. Becoming emotional when dealing with an already emotional group simply escalates hostility rather than defusing it.

RESOURCES

Borisoff, D., & Victor, D. (1998). *Conflict management: A communication skills approach*. Boston, MA: Allyn and Bacon.

Champagne, D., & Hogan, R. (1982). *Consultant supervisor theory and skill development*. Pittsburgh, PA: University of Pittsburgh Press.

Ellis, A., & Lange, A. (1994). *How to keep people from pushing your buttons*. New York: Birch Lane Press.

Gatto, R. (1990). *Practical guide to effective presentation*. Pittsburgh, PA: GTA Press.

Pike, B., & Arch, D. (1999). *Dealing with difficult participants*. San Francisco, CA: Jossey-Bass/Pfeiffer.

Mentoring

Q How Can I Be a Successful Mentor?

MENTORING IS A PHILOSOPHY and development process that aims to enhance the ability of a junior-level employee through the teaching and role modeling of a seasoned senior-level employee. It can be used in a wide range of situations. Mentoring is the process of the experienced sharing wisdom with care and compassion with the less experienced. A mentor is a wise, trusted counselor, teacher, or advisor. Mentors can provide coaching, friendship, sponsorship, and support, as well as model behavior. Mentors do not evaluate; they help others develop through discussion and feedback.

Benefits of the Mentoring Relationship

When an experienced mentor works with an inexperienced protégé, the following benefits are derived.

Mentor Provides

- Coaching,
- Friendship,
- Sponsorship,
- A role model,
- A safe environment,
- Support, not evaluation, and
- A sense of direction.

Employee Receives

- Developmental assistance,
- Motivation, and
- Benefit of mentor's experience and knowledge.

Organization Receives

- Strengthened culture,
- Core values passed from generation to generation,
- Cohesiveness,
- Development of future leaders,
- Consistency, and
- Increased rate of employee retention.

When People Mentor Others, They

- Enhance their communication skills,
- Develop sensitivity toward work and interpersonal skills,
- Have the opportunity to rethink, feel, and re-experience the workplace as they did earlier in their careers, and
- Develop rapport with employees.

The Mentoring Process

The mentor's job is to:

- Create a safe and comfortable climate,
- Observe and discuss the mentee's interactions and work-related skills, and

- Provide adequate and appropriate feedback for the mentee.

When the mentoring process is successful, both the mentor and the mentee develop. Mentors need to discuss specifics concerning the mentee's personal vision, career and business objectives, strengths and qualities, anticipated changes, and future expectations.

Mentors might begin the relationship by asking the mentee to outline all of his or her professional accomplishments, what business functions were performed, performance achievement, level reached in the organization, and volunteer work. This exercise will help to establish a personal vision from which the mentor can guide the mentee.

There are three very important components of the mentoring relationship: *climate, support,* and *feedback.*

Climate

It is essential to create a warm and supportive environment. Part of this process is to develop yourself and the mentee through the development of skills and better self-understanding. The climate must be conducive to free and open discussion without ramifications. A confidential atmosphere must be created; guidelines for interaction should be established, such as how often to meet; strengths and weaknesses must be identified, as well as any desired corrective actions; communication and personality styles must be discussed; and technical and people skills can be identified. You must develop trust between you and the mentee. It is important that you be empathic and understanding.

The mentoring process is designed to develop the potential, gifts, and talents of the mentee to support the organization. Success comes through making the person more efficient and productive in a humane way. Be careful not to impose your style, personality, or mannerisms on the mentee. Your job is to help the mentee develop his or her own talents.

Support

Be a supportive sounding board. Don't tell; listen. Your job is to pull out ideas, not push them in. Give the mentee the freedom to develop. Help him or her implement an action plan and give suggestions when asked. Ask questions to develop a clear picture of the mentee's feelings. Ask the mentee to write a report describing all of the things that he or she wants to accomplish professionally and personally. Include all the skills he or she will have enhanced, improved, or developed. Have the person describe business development and work specialization, career development, volunteer work, areas of interest, and community work. When complete, the report should identify goals to be achieved. Ask the mentee to consider how he or she will accomplish these goals and then write a plan of action leading toward these goals.

Feedback

Giving feedback is a way to help the mentee focus, learn, and grow from past experiences. The feedback process, a valuable tool in many other areas within the workplace, is especially important to the mentoring process.

When giving feedback, *focus* on the following:

Focus—key issues

Opportunities for development

Care—empathy—concern—compassion

Understanding and unconditional acceptance

Strengths

You also need to be aware that some mentees may have any or all of the following reactions (at different times) before accepting your feedback. By understanding these reactions, you can help the mentee reach the point of acceptance.

Reaction	Mentee	Mentor
Astonished	You can't mean me!	Let's review this and I can help you to understand how I came to this conclusion. Why are you surprised at this feedback?

Reaction	Mentee	Mentor
Anger	You do mean me!	Yes. Why don't you think about this for awhile and we can meet tomorrow to discuss it. (OR) You seem upset. Let's talk about this feedback.
Abandon	You can't be serious!	I know it may seem strange to you, but let's look at it and see how you can turn it into something positive. You seem to want to reject or resist accepting this feedback.
Acceptance	You are serious!	Yes, but we will work on it together.

When a mentee receives feedback, he or she may go through all four stages, but not necessarily. Whatever happens, it is important that he or she ends by accepting the feedback.

Key Areas of Development

The mentoring process is fulfilled by the mentee demonstrating development in key, observable ways. Such demonstrations of learning are essential to growth in the workplace. Discussing knowledge, technical ability, application, skills, attitude, and values will help guide a mentee's development. Here are some questions under each of these categories:

Knowledge. What is the person's general background? What was his or her field of study? What experiences has he or she had? How does the person interact with other employees, with peers, with upper management?

Technical Ability. How well does the person know his or her job? Does the person know how to do his or her direct reports' jobs and job-related aspects from other departments?

Application. How well does the mentee demonstrate his or her knowledge on a day-to-day basis? Is he or she able to get the job done?

Skills. Think of specific skills—role play manager/employee, manager/boss interactions with the mentee. Discuss skills and how the mentee perceives and performs these skills: communication, leadership, resolving conflict, building trust.

Attitude. What is the attitude of the mentee when working with others? What level of effort does the mentee exhibit and how does he or she act while in the work environment?

Values. What are the deep-seated beliefs of the mentee and what do they represent? How are they perceived by you and others?

Behavioral Skills

How you interact with the mentee is important if you are to build a solid, collaborative relationship. The following general skills need to be demonstrated by both the mentor and the mentee.

Building Self-Esteem

By reinforcing or enhancing an employee's self-esteem, the mentor taps into the self-motivation of the mentee. Treating a mentee with respect and as a competent person allows you to create mutual trust and a desire to improve performance.

Being Specific

Refer to events, time, acts, conditions, and people in measurable or specific terms. Specific references and measurable data clarify objectives, establish criteria, and define problems. Being specific leads the mentee to solutions, commits him or her to follow-up actions, and verifies your impressions to improve the quality of decisions and communications.

Listening Actively

Ask questions, listen, paraphrase, and establish mutual understanding. In general, employees spend 60 to 75 percent of their time meeting and communicating with others. Their achievements largely depend on how effectively they use this time. Effective communication is more than talking clearly. It involves strong listening skills that help to create mutual understanding of what has taken place or what is expected.

Resolving Issues

Establish a consistent fact-finding train of thought and seek input, data, and commitment before reaching a conclusion. The abilities to resolve issues, make decisions, and solve problems are the critical skills associated with a manager's position. The problem-solving and decision-making processes include differentiating types of problems, defining relevant data, establishing criteria, sorting issues, developing alternatives, involving the appropriate people, implementing an effective action plan, and following up to assure completion of all tasks.

Establishing Accountability

Set specific goals, develop action plans and a measurement system, monitor progress, provide management feedback, and reinforce accomplishments to improve performance. Effective employees establish a system of accountability and follow-up to connect setting goals with achieving results. It is a process that (a) systematically measures progress toward goals, (b) demonstrates to direct reports personal commitment to goal attainment, (c) reinforces good performance, and (4) identifies problems before they become major issues. It is the sense of accountability, recognition of the need to change, and desire to achieve goals that motivate people to higher performance levels. The mentee needs to demonstrate accountability throughout the mentoring process. This is a fundamental part of his or her development.

Summary

The mentoring process is meant to be a celebration of talent development. Use common sense. Remember that your job is to help the mentee discover issues rather than being told about them. Pull out talent and potential and help the mentee maintain and develop the skills that are appropriate for success. As you develop the mentee through this process, you will also be developing your own talents as a guide and mentor.

RESOURCES

Ambrose, L. (1998). *Mentor's companion.* Chicago, IL: Perrone-Ambrose Associates.

Fournies, F. (1987). *Coaching for improved work performance.* New York: McGraw-Hill.

Gatto, R. (1999). *Personal mentoring guide.* Unpublished manuscript. Gatto Training Associates, 733 Washington Road, Pittsburgh, PA 15228.

Ragins, B.R., & Cotton, J.L. (1999). Mentor functions and outcomes: A comparison of men and women in formal and informal mentoring relationships. *Journal of Applied Psychology, 84*(4), 529–550.

Q What Are the Phases of the Mentoring Process?

FOUR DEVELOPMENTAL STEPS are contained in the mentoring process. To complete the process successfully, a mentee should move through all four. These phases are *initiation, cultivation, separation,* and *autonomy.*

Initiation

The initiation phase lasts six months to one year as the relationship begins and the mentor and mentee are getting to know one another.

Key Development Points

- Direction of development is clarified;
- Goals and expectations are agreed on;
- Openness is developed; effective communication is established;
- Mentor supports mentee; mentee questions and takes responsibility for his or her development; and

- Interaction is on development of work-related and people-related skills.

Cultivation

This stage can last from one year to five years. During this period, the mentee develops his or her skills to the fullest.

Key Development Points

- Both the mentor and mentee benefit from the relationship;
- Mentee demonstrates implementation and development of skills;
- Trust and openness are fully developed; and
- Mentee takes responsibility for personal and professional growth.

Separation

This phase can last three to six months after the mentee and mentor agree that the mentee has developed sufficient self-confidence in his or her skills. Mentee develops self-recognition and the mentor receives feedback from others on mentee's development.

Key Development Points

- Mentee feels a need to work autonomously;
- Mentor recognizes mentee's need for autonomy;
- Mentee is ready to assume larger job responsibility and advances to more opportunity; and
- Mentee's goals and expectations are met.

Autonomy

The autonomous phase is an undefined period of time after the mentee/mentor relationship ends.

Key Development Points

- Mentor relationship is no longer necessary;
- Mentee can feel comfortable in coming back to the mentor if needed;
- Mentee is ready to be a mentor;
- Mentee is recognized for newly developed skills; and
- Mentee is comfortable in self-mentoring for development and continued growth.

RESOURCES

Ambrose, L. (1998). *Mentor's companion.* Chicago, IL: Perrone-Ambrose Associates.

Fournies, F. (1987). *Coaching for improved work performance.* New York: McGraw-Hill.

Gatto, R. (1999). *Personal mentoring guide.* Unpublished manuscript. Gatto Training Associates, 733 Washington Road, Pittsburgh, PA 15228.

Ragins, B.R., & Cotton, J.L. (1999). Mentor functions and outcomes: A comparison of men and women in formal and informal mentoring relationships. *Journal of Applied Psychology, 84*(4), 529–550.

How Can I Use a Mentee Development Plan?

BEFORE BEGINNING any mentor/mentee relationship, it is necessary to have a development plan in place. The development plan will give both the mentor and the mentee a starting point for their relationship and can be updated as the mentee progresses.

To create a development plan, the mentor and mentee should take the following steps at their first meeting.

- Complete skills assessment (see list of potential skill areas on pages 176–179).

- Discuss and reach agreement on mentee's present skill level for each skill dimension, using the first meeting to establish a baseline.

- Outline strengths and areas to work on.

- Write a development plan (see sample on pages 175–176).

- Agree on three to five skills that are strengths and reasons why the mentee is successful.

- Agree on three to five skills that are areas for development and what actions the mentee needs to undertake to develop and demonstrate the skill.
- Determine the priorities of the individual mentoring skills to be worked on.
- Agree on corrective action.
- Complete the developmental plan; both mentee and mentor initial; both keep copies.
- Identify and describe special assignment/client projects, building a relationship with a key partner or manager.
- If possible, meet for an update once a month informally (lunch or brief meeting).

At subsequent meetings, the mentor and mentee should complete the following steps.

- Review and discuss each mentoring skill not mentioned in the developmental plan.
- Review and discuss the three to five strengths and areas for development and corrective actions that were taken.
- Make necessary agreed-on adjustments to the plan.
- Review status and measure progress in development plan.
- Do a final review to reflect actual accomplishments.

Mentee Development Plan Outline

Below is an example of an outline the can be followed in developing a mentee plan.

Mentee Development Plan

Name: _____ Date: _____

List in priority order the skills (maximum of 3) to be improved on this year:

Identified Skill	Skill Rating	
	Initial	Ending

1. _____ _____ _____

Comment: _____
_____
_____

Action Planned: _____
_____
_____

Review Notes: _____
_____
_____

Completion Date: _____

Identified Skill	Skill Rating	
	Initial	Ending

2. _____ _____ _____

Comment: _____
_____
_____

Action Planned: _____
_____
_____

Review Notes: _____
_____
_____

Completion Date: _____

Identified Skill	Skill Rating	
	Initial	Ending

3. _____ ___ ___

Comment: _____
_____
_____

Action Planned: _____
_____
_____

Review Notes: _____
_____
_____

Completion Date: _____

Mentee Skills

The following list contains a variety of skills that the mentor and mentee may agree to work on in the mentoring relationship.

Client Relationship

- Is organized;
- Creates clear work papers;
- Meets client expectations;
- Follows through with client needs; and
- Maintains good client working relationships.

Communication

- Provides a steady, reliable flow of information internally and with clients;
- Actively listens and follows through;
- Runs effective, efficient, and informative meetings;
- Has clear and concise speaking and writing skills; and
- Is approachable.

Interpersonal Relationships

- Builds client rapport;
- Treats people fairly with respect and dignity;
- Is respectful of diversity in the workforce;
- Builds strategic relationships with key people;
- Is persuasive in helping others to see his/her perspective; and
- Is an effective and persuasive negotiator.

Leadership

- Is willing to help or assist others;
- Is trustworthy;
- Recognizes people for their accomplishments;
- Is looked up to as a positive role model;
- Is able to convince others to lend support and take action;
- Is a respected leader who is effective at managing conflict;
- Sets high standards for self and others; and
- Is nonjudgmental working with others.

Planning/Organization

- Clearly establishes clients' plan or process;
- Sets realistic and challenging goals and objectives;
- Defines plans so everyone knows what his or her accountabilities or responsibilities are;
- Organizes work so people understand the overall plan;
- Checks progress and adjusts goals periodically; and
- Makes effective use of time and available resource.

Problem Solving/Decision Making

- Readily assesses client problems and their impact;
- Uses collaborative decision making when appropriate;
- Seeks the input of others;
- Actively evaluates risks and benefits; and
- Focuses on timely action, not just on analysis.

Computer Technology

- Has attained required proficiency of assigned computer hardware and software; and
- Maintains proficiency with updated software.

Community/Professional Involvement

- Participates in professional organizations; and
- Represents the firm in various community functions/organizations.

Professional Presence

- Has a professional image;
- Represents the organization in a professional manner;
- Projects a positive organizational image;
- Works within the organization's values and beliefs;
- Builds on the legacy of the organization's reputation;
- Defines goals that further the organization's professional ability;
- Does not complain about the organization or others; and
- Dresses and displays demeanor that is appropriate for the occasion.

Initiative

- Continually re-evaluates internal plans to update and improve them;
- Routinely assesses competitive strategies looking for new opportunities;
- Makes follow-up calls and visits designed to exceed clients' expectations; and
- Displays a strong personal empowerment.

Innovation/Creativity

- Creatively works with clients;
- Encourages and brings new ideas;

- Anticipates opportunities for creativity;
- Encourages creative actions by others; and
- Helps others see alternative opportunities.

Accountability

- Is willing to be held accountable;
- Does not shift blame for own mistakes;
- Maintains loyalty to the organization; and
- Is truthful; does not hide mistakes.

Flexibility/Adaptability

- Is able to adapt/makes flexible plans to optimize results while maintaining focus on goals;
- Copes well with stress of changing priorities of tasks; and
- Sets the example for adapting to change.

Self-Directed

- Effectively works independently on assignments when required; and
- Displays common sense and practical application of knowledge and skills.

Motivation/Teamwork

- Creates a spirit of teamwork in his/her role in the organization;
- Uses appropriate recognition and rewards (says thank you);
- Accepts challenging responsibilities and engagements;
- Expresses interest in others;
- Mobilizes others to turn ideas into reality;
- Asks for and provides support to colleagues; and
- Completes client engagements in a timely fashion.

In addition, the mentee may wish to work on skills or knowledge specific to his or her job.

The mentor and mentee should review the mentee skills and decide together which skills to begin to work on. They can identify both skills and areas to be developed. They can then begin to work together to enhance the strengths and expand the areas to be developed.

RESOURCES

Ambrose, L. (1998). *Mentor's companion.* Chicago, IL: Perrone-Ambrose Associates.

Fournies, F. (1987). *Coaching for improved work performance.* New York: McGraw-Hill.

Gatto, R. (1999). *Personal mentoring guide.* Unpublished manuscript. Gatto Training Associates, 733 Washington Road, Pittsburgh, PA 15228.

Ragins, B.R., & Cotton, J.L. (1999). Mentor functions and outcomes: A comparison of men and women in formal and informal mentoring relationships. *Journal of Applied Psychology, 84*(4), 529–550.

 # Motivation

How Can I Motivate Myself?

MOTIVATION COMES ABOUT THROUGH an individual's thoughts, attitudes, and perceptions, which cause the person to be energized, wanting and desiring to put out effort in attaining a goal or objective. As each person has an individual thumbprint, so do we have individual reasons and rationales for the level of effort we demonstrate. Each individual must examine his or her own thoughts and attitudes to understanding what causes motivation. The twenty-five statements below are some of the more popular reasons people give for being motivated. People who are motivated have a tendency to be more productive, demonstrate more self-initiative, and achieve their goals. Take this motivational profile or give it to others as you wish.

Motivational Profile

Instructions: Read the statements below and put an "S" in front of the *five* items that best describe your greatest *strengths* and a "C" in front of the *five* items that best describe your five greatest *concerns.*

____	1. I am creative in my job.
____	2. I feel appreciated at work.
____	3. I have a good working rapport with my supervisor/ manager.
____	4. I have a sense of affiliation with my working associates.
____	5. I know my family supports my working career.
____	6. I feel I am appropriately recognized for my work.
____	7. I am challenged at work.
____	8. I have an opportunity to develop my talents at work.
____	9. I interact well with others at work.
____	10. I accept myself, realizing my potential and abilities.
____	11. I give myself credit for my successes.
____	12. I express my ideas openly.
____	13. I have been praised for my work.
____	14. I build trust with others.
____	15. I support others in their attempts to succeed.
____	16. I know what I want to achieve in the next five years.
____	17. I know what change is needed and how to achieve it.
____	18. I can fulfill my job responsibilities.
____	19. I help to create a relaxed environment.
____	20. I have a good working rapport with direct reports.
____	21. I understand my associates' needs.
____	22. I motivate myself at work.
____	23. I know who I am and what I want.
____	24. I receive appropriate compensation for my work.
____	25. I feel physically healthy.

Analyzing Your Motivational Profile

Instructions: List your five greatest strengths under the High Motivation heading below and your five greatest concerns under the Low Motivation heading. Now compare what motivates or causes you to put forth effort (high motivation) and what demotivates you or inhibits you from putting forth effort (low motivation).

High Motivation

1. _____
2. _____
3. _____
4. _____
5. _____

Low Motivation

1. _____
2. _____
3. _____
4. _____
5. _____

After you have finished this exercise, you should be able to recognize what motivates you in the future. You can now develop a personal motivation plan to maintain a high level of motivation. Think of the following equation: performance = ability x effort.

RESOURCES

Gatto, R. (1998). *Motivational profile.* Gatto Training Associates, 733 Washington Road, Pittsburgh, PA 15228.

How Can I Motivate My Direct Reports?

AS A MANAGER YOU ALSO need to recognize your direct reports for their good performance on the job. Recognition is a powerful motivator for continued performance at a high level. If you don't recognize or praise your direct reports, chances are they are not now nor ever will be motivated to perform at a top level. To become aware of whether you recognize the work of your direct reports in an appropriate way, complete the following assessments.

Why I Don't Praise

Instructions: Make a check mark below to identify any of your reasons for not praising employees.

_____ 1. I don't have time.

_____ 2. I have high expectations.

_____ 3. I do a lot, and I expect others to do a lot.

_____ 4. Employees need to be reminded how to improve and correct their work productivity; they can always improve.

_____ 5. I have difficulty expressing my feelings to employees.

_____ 6. I don't like to praise.

_____ 7. Other managers don't praise employees.

_____ 8. I don't think you should praise employees for doing their jobs.

_____ 9. I have too much to do.

_____ 10. My boss doesn't praise me, so I don't praise others.

_____ 11. The company culture doesn't promote praise of employees.

_____ 12. Other:

Why I Do Praise

Instructions: Use a check mark to identify any of the reasons below for why you praise or would want to praise employees.

_____ 1. To recognize an employee for a job well done.

_____ 2. Because the employee performed a quality job and completed it quickly and correctly.

_____ 3. Because the employee solved a problem on his or her own.

_____ 4. Because the employee provided extra service.

_____ 5. Because the employee is sensitive to others' needs.

_____ 6. Because the employee is a team player—loyal and supportive.

_____ 7. Because the employee is a motivated self-starter.

_____ 8. Because the employee accomplished a difficult or unusual job requirement.

_____ 9. Because the employee is an example for others.

_____ 10. As an incentive to the employee.

_____ 11. Because the employee is a steady, competent employee who fulfills work-related responsibilities.

_____ 12. Other:

If you find that you have more check marks in the "don't praise" list than in the "praise" list, you are probably not praising enough. Every item in the "praise" assessment is a valid reason for recognizing a direct report. Try to praise your direct reports each time one accomplishes one of these items.

Employees are motivated when they feel that what they are doing is worthwhile or is something they can believe in. By praising, you can reinforce these positive motivators. Look for ways to motivate employees in the following ways:

- Acknowledge the employee for doing something right. Have a meeting on success, not just problems or failure.

- If you want to know what motivates someone, ask.

- Don't view success as an expectation; reward effort and the right behavior.

- Don't view associates as an extension of yourself. They are different; their working styles, attitudes, and values are not yours. Your expectations of workers should be individualized. What motivates you may not be what motivates others.

- Be honest; avoid threats or punishments.

- Praise associates from their points of view, not yours as the manager. If an associate deserves praise, express it in personal and specific terms, for example: *"We appreciate the work you have done on. . ."* or *"We realize the effort you have . . ."* not, *"This has benefited me."*
- Give praise and credit when it is due and appropriate.
- Step back and analyze the work you and associates are doing (sometimes we can't see the *trees* for the *forest*). Remember the *individual.*
- Don't forget about the average performer, the associate who consistently performs every day, who is *not* a bright star and probably won't be promoted, but is an integral part of the working team. Find a way to praise these people.
- After praise, avoid, "You should have . . ."; "Next time . . ."; "This was great; do this more often"; "Okay, but I would have done it. . . ."

Remember that an employee is motivated: (1) when he or she trusts and respects the supervisor or manager, (2) when the job is important and an extension of the individual's abilities, values, and challenges, and (3) when the supervisor or manager gives sincere, honest, realistic, and deserved praise. Employees are motivated when they feel they have an opportunity to demonstrate their ability. It is especially important to remember that the behaviors rewarded today are the behaviors that employees will develop for tomorrow.

RESOURCES

Blanchard, K., & Zigarmi, D. (1985). *Leadership and the one minute manager.* New York: William Morrow.

Drucker, P. (1999). *Management challenges for the 21st century.* New York: HarperCollins.

Gatto, R. (1992). *Teamwork through flexible leadership.* Pittsburgh, PA: GTA Press.

Nelson, B. (1994). *1001 ways to reward employees.* New York: Workman.

Performance Appraisal

Q

What Is the Appropriate Way to Praise or Reprimand an Employee?

EVERYONE NEEDS PRAISE and, when the occasion calls for it, a reprimand. Both can be motivational events. The following are steps for appropriate employee praise and reprimand within the context of performance appraisal. Praise offers recognition; reprimands present alternatives. If goals have not been clearly established, or a policy or procedure is not clear, then praise and reprimand lose their meaning.

1. State the issue(s), problem(s), event(s): "I would like to discuss. . . ."

2. Identify and focus on the facts and issues, not on the person. Discuss event(s), behavior, and performance. Be specific: "The other day you. . . ."

3. Discuss the results from the event, behavior, and performance. Be specific: "As a result of. . . ."

4. Tell the employee how you feel about what he or she did or said. Focus on the person's action(s). Don't make comparisons with other employees. Each employee

needs to hear from you what is or is not appropriate within the workplace. "I feel that you. . . ."

5. Listen to the employee without rebuttal.

Following are several examples of situations of when to praise and when to reprimand.

Praise

- Successful completion of any project;
- When something is completed satisfactorily;
- When completion is on time and within budget; and
- When an employee continues to aid and support a project.

Reprimand

- When there is poor performance;
- When the employee needs to know what he or she did wrong in order to further his or her development; and
- When corrective actions need to be demonstrated.

When reprimanding, it is important to focus on facts and to provide alternative behaviors. Praise should be given not just in formal performance appraisals, but whenever a task, however small, is successfully completed.

RESOURCES

Cascio, W. (1995, November). Whither industrial and organizational psychology in a changing world of work. *American Psychologist, 50*(11), 928–939.

Fournies, F. (1987). *Coaching for improved work performance.* New York: McGraw-Hill.

Nelson, B. (1994). *1001 ways to reward employees.* New York: Workman.

Q How Can I Conduct an Effective Performance Appraisal?

A PERFORMANCE APPRAISAL gives an employee and his or her supervisor an opportunity to assess the employee's level of accomplishment as demonstrated through performance on the job. By conducting periodic performance appraisals, a manager gives employees information about their present levels of job performance, allows them to agree on expected levels of job performance for the future, and informs them of the actions needed to achieve success in the job performance. The performance appraisal is meant to be a developmental process for the employee. It needs to focus the employee on him- or herself and on the utilization of talent and effort. The performance appraisal should not be used for comparing employees to one another, nor as a method to distribute money.

Performance appraisals can be organized into three phases:

Phase I—Set the Ground Rules

- Mutually establish and agree on realistic goals and align goals to business objectives.

- Establish the appropriate amount of time to accomplish the goals.

Phase II—Give Feedback

- Focus on actions, not the person or emotions.
- Listen. Ask the associate to describe his or her effort toward achieving the goal; add your perception of the person's effort toward accomplishing the goal.
- Don't criticize. Give supportive and corrective feedback.
- Compare the agreed-on goal with the associate's motivation, skills, and accomplishments. Divide accomplishments between work-related and people-oriented.
- Exchange ideas for building toward the future. Don't dwell on the past.

Phase III—Plan Development

- Identify strengths and opportunities for development.
- Conclude: "What goals do we agree on? What is your commitment to following through?"

What a Performance Appraisal Does

A performance appraisal clearly establishes *what is expected* (job responsibilities), thereby establishing criteria for acceptable and unacceptable work performance within a specified time frame. A performance appraisal focuses on responsibilities to be fulfilled, rather than on tasks to be completed. The employee receiving feedback from a performance appraisal should see it as both a developmental challenge and a learning experience. The performance appraisal should help the employee receiving feedback strive to use his or her talents, abilities, and skills.

A clearly defined performance appraisal process enables everyone to identify what is expected on the job. It allows employees to discuss supportive and/or corrective action (opportunities for development) and establish a plan of action so job expectations and work performance become aligned.

Providing Feedback

Open, honest, respectful communication is necessary to build a trusting relationship. The performance appraisal should track the employee's development. Performance appraisals should be used as an individual measure and not as a measure between or among employees. The appraisal and the forms are confidential between the manager and individual employee only.

In writing general statements about performance, wording should be simple, clear, and to the point. Write factually without emotion or bias to the best of your ability. You lessen bias and emotion by identifying and being aware of the chance for these reactions before the performance appraisal and while writing your assessment.

When writing corrective and supportive feedback, clearly explain your rationale. Use word descriptors such as "(in)appropriate" or "(un)satisfactorily completed" and "(un)professional manner" ("performed assignments in a(n) (un)professional manner with Company A by . . . ." "appropriately fulfilled (met) job responsibilities during the quarter as demonstrated by. . . [or] as evidenced by . . . . . ."). Other word descriptors include "will be held accountable to. . . [or] answerable for. . . [or] duty to perform. . . [or] function as a . . . [or] required to . . . [or] obligation to. . . ." State expectations for the employee.

Elements of a Performance Appraisal

A performance appraisal is usually successful if the following elements and attitudes are present:

1. Job performance is seen as an observable and measurable act toward fulfilling job responsibilities, as interpreted and agreed on by employee and manager.

2. Quality of performance is seen as taking time, effort, commitment, and follow-up.

3. Through assessing and supporting performance, traditions and standards develop and can be sustained.

4. Follow-up on performance appraisal must take place more than once a year because:

   Responsibilities may change or be altered (economics; goals; changes; priorities; business objectives).

   Continually establishing an agreement on performance is mutually beneficial.

   Such discussions establish rapport through collaboration; working together develops mutual understanding, trust, and respect, and clarifies goals.

   Reinforcing performance appraisal and treating employees with respect helps them take responsibility for their own actions.

5. A high level of trust exists among peers, employees, and managers.

6. The appraisal is perceived to be a fair (equitable) and accurate measure of performance.

7. The performance appraisal form is available to the employee.

8. Employees perceive that they have some input into the performance appraisal system.

9. Employees perceive the system to be developmental and supportive of their professional growth.

10. A method exists to demonstrate accomplishments.

11. A supportive environment is created that ensures confidentiality and encourages and stimulates discussion through supportive and corrective feedback, note taking, and follow-up action.

12. Business outcomes (results) are established.

13. The process involves all employees and develops strategy and vision.

14. The process seeks to understand all viewpoints.

15. The process meets organizational, associates,' and the manager's needs.

Giving a Performance Appraisal

A performance appraisal should start with a discussion on the following:

- Job responsibilities;
- Activities the employee will fulfill;
- Work-related and people-related activities;
- Outline of personal characteristics of the employee to fulfill the position;
- Alignment of responsibilities with business objectives;
- Explanation of the relationship between the employee fulfilling responsibilities and the manager fulfilling responsibilities; and
- Explanation of growth, learning, and development for the employee.

Organizations need to have a quick response time to situations and be flexible to change. To achieve this, the performance appraisal system must be process-based rather than task-based. Outlining responsibilities that are to be fulfilled rather than simply listing tasks is an important part of developing process-based organizations. A performance appraisal system can be very helpful here.

The following is an example of a performance appraisal used in a business corporation. You may want to tweak it to suit your own department's needs and then use it with your employees.

Sample Performance Appraisal

Person Being Evaluated: _____

Today's Date: _____

Please check one:

__Self-Assessment __Boss __Peer __Direct Report __Other

Instructions: Circle the level that best represents the performance abilities of the person listed above, using the following continuum.

	High				Low
1. Level at which person performs job responsibilities	5	4	3	2	1
2. Flexibility while working with others	5	4	3	2	1
3. Listening ability	5	4	3	2	1
4. Oral communication ability	5	4	3	2	1
5. Written communication ability	5	4	3	2	1
6. Ability to create trust with others	5	4	3	2	1
7. Level of confidence in job performance	5	4	3	2	1
8. Ability to take appropriate and timely action	5	4	3	2	1
9. Work-related knowledge	5	4	3	2	1
10. Ability to work effectively with others	5	4	3	2	1
11. Ability to resolve conflict	5	4	3	2	1
12. Ability to make timely decisions	5	4	3	2	1
13. Ability to problem solve	5	4	3	2	1
14. Ability to set goals and follow through	5	4	3	2	1
15. Ability to organize the work load and set clear priorities	5	4	3	2	1
16. Work ethic	5	4	3	2	1

Comments:
Performance Strengths:

Opportunities for Development:

Summary

The performance appraisal should be ongoing, not a one-time event. It is a *diagnosis* and *prescription* process that an employee helps to develop and is held accountable to fulfill. It is the employee's responsibility to demonstrate the performance.

Many times the performance appraisal creates anxiety on the part of both the rater and the employee and becomes nothing more than an appeasement process. However, a well-operated and respected performance appraisal system can be a method to create growth and recognition for the organization, as well as the people involved.

RESOURCES

Brinkerhoff, R., & Messinger, R. (1999). *Strategic employee development guide*. San Francisco, CA: Jossey-Bass/Pfeiffer.

Cascio, W. (1995, November). Whither industrial and organizational psychology in a changing world of work. *American Psychologist, 50*(11), 928–939.

Fournies, F. (1987). *Coaching for improved work performance*. New York: McGraw-Hill.

Murphy, K.R., & Cleveland, J.N. (1995). *Understanding performance appraisal*. Thousand Oaks, CA: Sage.

Smither, J. (1998). *Performance appraisal*. San Francisco, CA: Jossey-Bass.

Presentation Skills

How Can I Design an Effective Presentation?

DURING THE COURSE of your career, you will probably have to give presentations—to customers, to peers, to direct reports, and to management. Preparation not only lessens anxiety, but also produces a more effective presentation. Designing a presentation may seem like a huge responsibility, but by following the steps below, it can become a manageable, and even enjoyable, task. Think of the brain as though it were like the stomach, in that you put one bite of food in your mouth at a time. Information in a presentation is brain food, one thought at a time. Here is a presentation motto: you can do more with less.

Pre-Presentation Questions

- What do I want to accomplish? Why am I speaking—to inform or to persuade?
- To whom am I speaking? Define your audience's needs.
- How long should I speak?

Visuals

- You are a visual, so be aware of dress and facial expressions.
- Visuals should be self-explanatory.
- Plan to distribute handouts (usually before the presentation; during the presentation if needed; and after if needed or as a reinforcement).

The Presentation

- Meet your audience; collect names if possible.
- Introduce yourself if needed.
- Presentations should have three parts:
  - Overview—What you are going to present: (title), purpose; objectives: what, why, to whom; benefits to the people/organization/customer; ground rules; topics.
  - Body—Facts that support your overview.
  - Summary—Emphasize key points.

Post-Presentation Questions

- Did you accomplish what you wanted?
- Did you meet your audience's needs?
- Is there a need for follow-up action?

Now that you have studied an overview of the presentation, you have some idea of what is expected for the entire process. Below are the components that make up the presentation itself.

Building Your Presentation

Daydream, formulate ideas, write a theme, write general topics, and outline your thoughts into an overview, body, and summary.

Overview

The overview should inform the audience of all the topics to be presented. Think of three main points you want the audience to walk away with. After the overview, there should be no surprises in your presentation. Your overview should contain the following:

- What will be discussed;
- No more than three main points/topics;
- Outline of topics;
- Grabber, that is, what the audience should remember, what is beneficial for them;
- Ground rules, for example, that people may or may not ask questions during your presentation; whether handouts will be used; and break and lunch times.
- Questions either will be used to gain information, in which case they can be asked at any time, or if you want to control and influence the audience, have them hold their questions until a specified time.

Body

The body of the presentation should flow smoothly from the overview. It should be logically organized. Large note cards with topic sentences can help you to keep thoughts (and the presentation) in order. Support the presentation with visual aids. Slides, PowerPoint®, overheads, flip charts, and so forth, will help the audience understand your message. Do not *read* your presentation!

Summary

The summary should reinforce the salient ideas of the presentation. Say, "In summary. . . ." The summary could also include questions of the audience regarding the main topics of the presentation and a recap of the key issues by the audience with your guidance. (However, questions and answers could occur anywhere in your presentation and you could ask questions of the audience throughout your presentation.) Briefly present concepts or issues that you want the audience to remember and think about.

The following is a brief example of a presentation, with the outline on the left and script on the right.

Good Morning. I'm _____

This morning, I am going to present "Keys to Effective Presentations."

Purpose: My purpose today is to share a process for effectively and efficiently designing and giving a presentation.

Acknowledge the Audience: I realize that many in the audience already give presentations. This workshop will give you an approach to design your presentations more easily.

Benefits: By following this presentation format, you will be able to present your ideas clearly. By clearly presenting your ideas, you will help your audience understand the point of your presentation more easily. Your presentation will be efficient and focused. Customers will enjoy the focus of your presentation and your ability to customize your presentations to meet their needs.

Ground Rules: My presentation will be approximately twenty minutes. Please hold your questions until the end. The handout will be used for notes and/or explanation of material.

Topic: The two topics I will cover are:

1. Difference between influencing and informing.
2. Presentation design: overview, body, and summary.

(You can use the topic visual as a summary visual also.)

Body: The difference between influencing and informing.

- To inform is to state a law or inform about a policy.
- To influence is to have someone adopt your idea.

(Go on to give the rest of the presentation. Every time you design a presentation, write three or four questions on cards and use them to emphasize points during the presentation. Answer the questions, and then ask people to comment. This is an easy way to generate discussion, if that is what you want.)

Summary: Summarize, discuss, and clarify the differences between influencing and informing and the presentation design. State, "By following this format, we will. . . ."

In Conclusion: Today I discussed the difference between influencing and informing when designing a presentation. Thank you.

Key Issues for Presentations

Keep in mind the following eight concepts when preparing for a presentation.

1. Be well-informed and well-prepared.

    Present both the background and the newest concepts on the subject matter.

    Know the subject matter, but don't just memorize it and repeat it.

    Have general knowledge of a specific area and be able to explain, analyze, apply, and evaluate all of the facts that are presented.

    Explain subject matter as if you are dealing with a friendly colleague.

Start with an overview of general concepts and systematically explain specifics until you are satisfied that all of the content to be covered has been discussed.

2. Know in advance what the audience expects from your presentation.

   Research the needs of the audience by speaking with an informed source.

   If you do not know what the audience expects, ask questions to determine expectations, for example: "Before we begin, tell me what you personally expect from this presentation. Tell me what specific areas you would like to discuss."

   Remain flexible to meet the audience's needs.

3. To stay on track and within the allotted period of time, do the following:

   Prepare for a presentation by outlining all the major concepts to be covered.

   Use note cards to identify topic sentences and key points.

   Emphasize and sequence salient facts to promote understanding.

4. Draw the participants into the presentation with questions.

   Do not wait for questions; ask your own. As the presenter, try to generate a dialogue with your audience by asking for comments and calling on individuals. Have audience members relate experiences or comment on a question you raise.

   If possible, use name cards for the audience or ask each person to identify him- or herself by name and position before the presentation begins.

   Conduct small-group discussion to generate questions or solutions to problems.

   Do not let the audience passively sit by as you discuss ideas. To know what they are thinking or whether they are comprehending, you need to *ask questions,* involve the audience, and discuss.

5. You are a visual.

Be aware of your movements and remember that nervous gestures (pacing, clenching and unclenching hand, fussing with jewelry) distract from the content.

Good posture, strength in body movements, and eye contact greatly enhance your presentation. Effective speakers use body language to engage the audience.

If appropriate, you should sit so you are accepted as part of the audience or as a colleague.

Practice your presentation in front of a mirror.

It is important that you dress appropriately for your audience. Dress (appearance) can add credibility to you as a presenter.

6. Use your voice as an instrument.

Change the pace of the presentation. For example, to highlight different, specific, or important facts, speak slowly and loudly.

Pauses can be used after an important thought for emphasis.

7. The presentation should stay within the allotted time.

Repetition may be necessary to highlight salient points, but not to take up time.

If you can conclude a presentation earlier than the allotted time, do so. (You should quit before everyone knows what you are going to say next.)

For a one-hour presentation, prepare approximately forty-five minutes' worth. This will allow time for questions and clarification.

8. Use a brief summary to explain the overview and the specifics that were covered.

State, "In summary . . ." or "In conclusion . . ."

The final summary is extremely important. It should pull together all the facts and create a whole concept of what was presented.

If you want to stimulate discussion, break the audience into small groups to analyze a topic. (The audience usually does not ask questions without prompting.)

Review the checklist below before a presentation.

Presentation Checklist

____ Make eye contact with members of the audience.

____ Speak loudly, clearly; use appropriate pace.

____ Be enthusiastic—think about facial expression.

____ Don't pace or shift your weight.

____ Avoid fondling objects with your hands.

____ Pause—breathe slowly and deeply.

____ Don't be nervous—no one but you knows what's next.

____ Use the entire room.

____ Be aware of your posture.

____ Dress according to audience expectations.

____ Avoid ah's, uhm's, and you know's (use silence instead).

Evaluation

A good way to learn more about your strengths and weaknesses as a presenter is to ask a colleague to observe you and provide feedback. An observer can use a form such as the following to record impressions.

Presentation Assessment Report

Name: _____

A = Excellent   B = Satisfactory   C = Improvement Needed

Note to Evaluator: If a concept is not applicable, leave a blank.

Speaker

_____ eye contact

_____ speaking volume

_____ use of hands

_____ use of pauses

_____ completes thoughts

_____ appearance

_____ enthusiasm

_____ draws audience participation

_____ body movement

_____ use of the room

_____ use of pointer/ highlighter

_____ pace

Content

_____ overview

_____ body

_____ summary

_____ Q&A

_____ logical flow

Visuals

_____ facial expressions

_____ overhead transparencies

_____ video/slides

_____ flip chart

_____ handouts/follow-up

_____ overview/summary

Comments:

Instructions: Check any of the following roles the presenter assumed during the presentation.

_____ persuader/influencer   _____ informer

_____ parent to child   _____ experimenter

_____ authoritarian   _____ salesperson

_____ supervisor to subordinate

RESOURCES

Carnegie, D. (1955). *Public speaking and influencing men in business.* New York: Associated Press.

Gatto, R. (1990). *Effective presentation.* Pittsburgh, PA: GTA Press.

Yeomans, W.B. (1985). *1000 things you never learned in business school.* New York: McGraw-Hill.

How Can I Create Effective Visuals?

VISUALS ARE AN IMPORTANT TOOL when making presentations for two primary reasons: (1) they allow the audience to focus on the material and (2) they provide reinforcement for the spoken word.

A variety of visual tools are available, but here we will focus on the following: flip charts, transparencies, slides, and white boards.

Flip Charts

A list of helpful hints for using a flip chart follows:

1. Use a flip chart to introduce and set the tone for the presentation. The first page should feature the title of the presentation, the second your name and position (if appropriate).

2. Use a flip chart to display an outline of the presentation. You can use this chart in your summary too.

3. Use a flip chart to divide sections presenting new or different information. This helps the audience follow a change of topic. Limit wording on any sheet to one or two phrases.

4. Use a flip chart to clarify and support your presentation.

5. Use a flip chart to record the audience's responses to important questions or to note issues for later discussion. Post these pages on the wall in order to keep track of unresolved issues while guiding the presentation to a timely conclusion.

6. Prepare flip charts ahead of time. Also, a statement, logo, or definition could be posted before a presentation and taped to the wall for reference.

7. Make the information on the flip-chart pages stand out. Use bold, dark colors for titles or to emphasize a problem word or concept. Use blue, green, or black (darker colors) for general information; avoid light colors (yellows, pinks). Red letters usually indicate a problem.

8. When using a flip chart, *lightly write notes in pencil* next to ideas you have written in with a marker. Your penciled notes will only be visible to you. The audience's eyes will be drawn to the bright colors and you will have built a support system for yourself with your notes. Notes such as "eye contact" and "volume" will help you to remember your skills. Note content issues as well.

9. Stand to the side of the flip chart. Use your hand or a pointer to note each specific topic.

10. Use abbreviations and acronyms with care. If you think your audience will be confused, spell out terms on your flip charts. (When presenting to large groups, spell out any abbreviations or acronyms you'll be using in the handouts you distribute to audience members.)

11. Post the flip chart where everyone can see it.

12. Flip charts should be self-explanatory, with a title and information or a clear statement.

Overhead Transparencies/ Slides/PowerPoint® Shows

Read through the following list of hints before using transparencies, slides, or computer graphic shows.

1. Do not put too much information on your transparency or slide. Use large print and wide spacing. Screens filled with numbers usually do not convey what is intended. Use no more than six lines of bulleted text. Keep it simple.

2. Use bold, dark colors for titles or to emphasize a problem word or concept. Use blue, green, or black (darker colors) for general information; avoid light colors (yellows, pinks). Red letters usually indicate a problem.

3. Visuals should be self-explanatory, with a title and information or a clear statement.

4. When comparing information, put the points in columns across from each other, not on top of each other.

5. Clear transparencies can be produced on most copy machines. Use a colored transparency pen or colored tape for emphasis or to highlight salient points.

6. Use the top two-thirds of the screen for your data. This will keep the data higher on the screen and make it easier for the audience to see.

7. Always frame (mount) the transparency or purchase transparencies that have a white border. Use the frame to write notes to yourself and number them for display.

8. If possible, have transparencies you use often manufactured at a professional quick-print store. Computerized transparencies provide the most effective style.

9. Use a laser pointer to emphasize important information and to indicate which point you are talking about at a given time.

White Boards

The following hints will be useful for working on a white board.

1. Use a white board to outline or highlight a presentation in a conference room.
2. If possible, use colored pens and write neatly and in a large block letters.
3. Stand to the side and use a pointer to refer to particular topics within the outline. Underline important words.

Equipment

Be sure to read through the following list before using any type of equipment such as a projector or computer.

1. Before your presentation, check your equipment to make sure it is working. Remember Murphy's Law.
2. View all slides, transparencies, and so forth before the presentation, with the lights on and the lights off to note the effect.
3. Tighten the top of the slide carousel to prevent the slides from falling out. If a slide gets stuck, bend a paper clip into an "L" shape with a small bottom. Reach down and pull up the slide to disengage.

Presentation Kit

To be an effective presenter, you need to be able to meet the needs of a changing environment and audience. To properly meet this challenge carry a presentation kit containing the following items:

• Large paper clips;
• Masking tape to post flip-chart pages (and for repairs);
• Scissors;
• Rubber bands;

- Marking pens, both wide and fine point;
- Overhead transparencies and transparency pens;
- Pens and pencils with erasers;
- Stick pins to post flip-chart pages on felt or carpeted walls;
- A pointer that extends to about two feet, or a laser pen;
- A plug adapter (three- to two-prong);
- A stapler and staple remover;
- A stop watch;
- A calculator; and
- If you use slides, carry a small extension cord in the carousel box and an extra light bulb.

Graphics

Some of the most challenging visual elements for presenters are graphics. The purpose of graphics is to put out a great deal of information without needing to explain every detail. Graphics also compare, contrast, support, and present analysis. Let the audience view a graphic for five to fifteen seconds before you begin to explain it. When using a graph, present the audience with a brief explanation or assignment. For example, ask the audience how to apply the data on the graph. State the problem it represents and/or the function it serves. All graphs need to be clearly marked with appropriate titles, dates, and information. The simpler the better. Ask yourself these questions when creating your graphics:

1. Is the graphic colorful and easily readable?
2. Have I limited the amount of text on the graphic?
3. Can the graphic stand alone without an explanation? (A graphic must represent a complete concept independent of an oral description.)
4. Do I need to use a key to explain details?
5. Did I use color to aid in visual discrimination?

Four common graphic elements are described below.

Quadrant Graphs

Quadrant graphs are used to identify different products/characteristics, to analyze quality, and to show the relationship between two variables, as shown on the sample quadrant graph below.

Example: Management Style

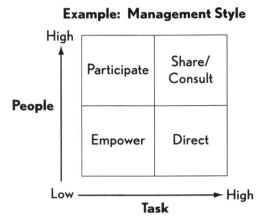

The sample graph shows the four leadership styles. The Direct style indicates high task and low people orientation. The Share/Consult style shows high people and high task orientation. The Participate style shows high people, low task orientation, and the Empower style shows low people and low task orientation. By looking at this visual, one can compare and contrast the interactions among the different variables. The relationship between task orientation, people orientation, and leadership styles is easily explained and understood through this quadrant graph.

Line Graphs

Use a line graph to show comparisons, individual growth analysis, sales results, or other individual factors. This visual can be used to break out the data over time or by source, rather than presenting a single number.

The purpose of the line graph is to demonstrate change or stability. The first example below shows a comparison of the number of deliveries of two products being sold over the last year. Product A sales can be compared with Product B sales. The second example shows the percentage of damaged product A and damaged product B over one year. The impact of this visual can support statements that you might make about these products in your presentation.

Number of Deliveries

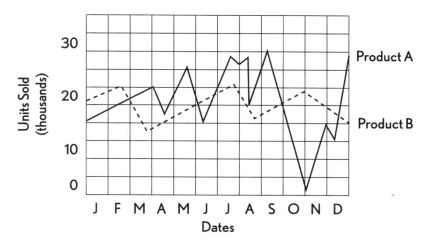

Percentage of Damaged Products

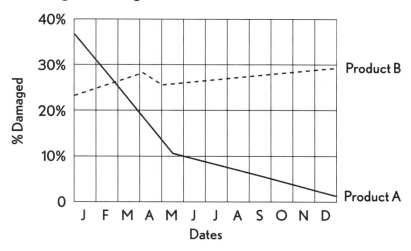

Pie Charts

The pie chart should be divided into slices, with each slice labeled and given a percentage. The total of all slices should equal 100 percent. This graphic should be used to measure individual components within the whole and to show their importance.

The example below shows the percentage of communication time spent on various modes of communication by an office staff. By looking at the chart, one can easily see that 50 percent of staff communication time is spent in meetings. This may lead senior management to evaluate meeting processes to make sure that this time is being well-spent.

Office Communication

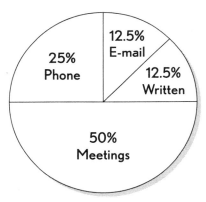

Bar Charts

Bar charts are used to show differences or compare two things. Bars can also be drawn to show change, improvement, or decline.

The first example below shows reasons for customer complaints during the month of January. It is obvious from looking at the bar chart that the biggest problem was late delivery. The second bar chart compares the sales of a given product each month over an entire year.

January Customer Complaints

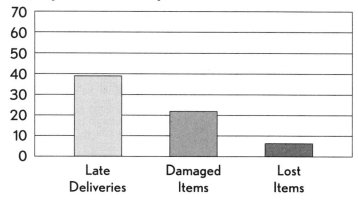

Change in Sales

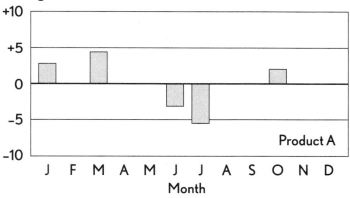

Visuals can play an important role in any presentation. Properly done, they can reinforce what has been said. They can also create a lasting impression of a particular point. Because people could be visual learners, rather than aural/oral learners, you will reach more of your audience by enhancing your presentation with graphic elements.

RESOURCES

Brandt, R.C. (1987). *Flip charts: How to draw them and how to use them.* San Francisco, CA: Jossey-Bass/Pfeiffer.

Burn, B.E. (1996). *Flip chart power.* San Francisco, CA: Jossey-Bass/Pfeiffer.

Gatto, R. (1990). *Effective presentation.* Pittsburgh, PA: GTA Press.

Wilder, C., & Fine, D. (1996). *Point, click, and wow!! A quick guide to brilliant laptop presentations.* San Francisco, CA: Jossey-Bass/Pfeiffer.

Problem Solving

What Method Can I Use to Define Problems?

WE OFTEN WANT to be creative and change the way we view problems. You can use the following alternative thinking model when dealing with issues around change and/or in breaking your mind-set in order to organize and define problems.

Developing Alternative Thinking

		Want	Don't Want
PRESENT	Have	**2** Maintain (Strength)	**3** Eliminate (Problem)
FUTURE	Don't Have	**1** Acquire (Future Direction)	**4** Avoid (Possible Pitfalls)

As shown, your problem can be broken down into present and future, want and don't want, have and don't have. Look at each aspect of your problem and decide what you want to keep and what you want to achieve. This technique can generate a lot of information and give you some different ways to view your problem. Below are the steps you can take to organize your ideas.

1. First, identify the problem. Actually write it out on a flip chart.

2. Collect viewpoints about the problem from the problem-solving participants.

3. Outline the present situation concerning the problem. Are there any positives within the situation? List them. Now, project to the future. List the future positives and anticipated problems if there is no change in the situation.

4. Look at what you can maintain and what you can eliminate. By maintaining, you can avoid something else (for example, if you maintain the present level of employment, you avoid layoffs).

5. Next, look at what you can acquire and what you can eliminate. By acquiring, you can eliminate something else (for example, to eliminate the lack of communication in the office, you can acquire informational meetings).

By using this technique, you can focus on the positives and negatives in a short period of time and make the entire process of problem solving more manageable. *Remember*: Every success helps you to learn what to do, what to maintain, and what to acquire. Every mistake helps you to learn what not to do, what to avoid, and what to eliminate. *Try it!*

Example: "How can we increase creativity?" What do you need to acquire, maintain, eliminate, and avoid? Generate your ideas under all four categories, as shown in the following example.

Acquire (Don't Have and Want) Future	Maintain (Have and Want) Present	Eliminate (Have; Don't Want)	Avoid (Don't Want; Don't Have)
More diverse customer base	A few strong customers	One poor customer who pays very late	Layoffs
New computer software system for control of products	Excellent product	Loss of material	Losing customers
	Excellent service		Poor service
Different level of employees	Present sales force	Poorly functioning equipment	Poor product development

This format helps to stimulate your ideas through asking four questions. From a *Present* point of view (what is occurring right now), what is being done correctly that needs to be *Maintained,* and what is being done incorrectly (problems) that needs to be *Eliminated?* From a *Future* perspective, what does one not have that needs to be *Acquired* and what does one not have nor want that needs to be *Avoided* (pitfalls, future problems)?

The purpose of process tools is to help you to expand your thinking. The creative process is essentially expanding beyond current knowledge to new ways of understanding by using new information. The model above will help you explore and expand your thinking.

RESOURCES

Carr, C. (1994). *The competitive power of constant creativity.* New York: AMACOM.

Gatto, R. (1992). *Teamwork through flexible leadership.* Pittsburgh, PA: GTA Press.

Greenberg, J., & Baron, R. (1997). *Behavior in organizations* (6th ed.). Upper Saddle River, NJ: Prentice Hall.

Van Gundy, A.B. (1988). *Techniques of structured problem solving* (2nd ed.). New York: Van Nostrand Reinhold.

Q How Can I Work Through a Problem?

IGNORING A PROBLEM sometimes seems to be the easiest way to deal with it. However, when a problem is not worked out, it can easily escalate into a crisis. It is far easier to deal with a problem in a calm, reflective manner, when you have time to discuss and reassess, than it is to be forced to deal with a crisis, for which solutions may be reactionary and not responsive to the actual issue. The model below shows steps to take to analyze and work through problems.

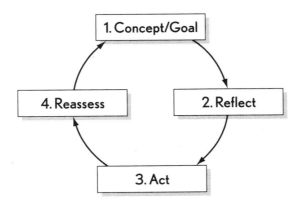

Here's how the model works:

1. *Concept/Goal.* The first step in determining how you'll tackle a problem is to develop a goal, that is, what you want to achieve by eliminating the problem. In order to reach your goal, collect data relevant to the *cause* of the problem, not just data about what is happening at the present time.

2. *Reflect.* Now is the time to brainstorm ideas. Don't limit yourself. Create strategies and explore methods for implementing your ideas.

3. *Act.* Implement your strategies or methodologies within a specific, realistic time frame. Be patient. Keep the momentum going once you begin by scheduling time to periodically reassess the implementation.

4. *Reassess.* Because no process is 100 percent foolproof, you'll want to assess your progress periodically. Although the model is linear, this review should actually occur at each step in the process.

Another problem-solving model is given in the seven steps below.

Seven Steps to Creative Problem Solving

1. *Define the problem.* Write your problem/statement, for example: "In our Purchasing Department, we don't seem to be able to communicate effectively, either externally or internally."

2. *Research and analyze.* If needed, redefine the problem.

3. *Generate ideas.* Focus on generating specific ideas. Put the problem on a visual (paper, white board) and draw a circle around it. Collect responses about the problem. Without criticizing any of the ideas, list anything even remotely related to the problem. Use the following format to hang your ideas onto the problem as you've defined it.

Poor
Communication
(Defined
Problem)

interruptions
lack of proper equipment
manager micromanages
lack of corporate commitment for change
technical problems
no communication between departments
manager acts without communicating
financial problems
oversharing information
no clear method for dealing with customer calls
short time frame to produce results
leadership problems
expectations unclear

4. *Evaluate ideas and prioritize them.* After you have
   written all the ideas you have, prioritize them by how
   pertinent they are to the goal you want to achieve.
   Write them in two lists: high priorities and low priorities, as shown below.

High Priorities	Low Priorities
Inform other departments	Interruptions
Technical problems/ corporate commitment	Short time frame to produce results

5. *Develop and implement a strategy.* After you have
   selected the high-priority items, you need to develop a
   plan to address them. The plan should outline individual actions with specific details, examine all available
   resources and the level of motivation, and consider any
   obstacles. What could prevent implementation? Identify
   your concerns and solicit the concerns of others about
   the problem.

Choose one of the priorities and develop a solution for it. For example, one of the high-priority items from our example was "inform other departments." A plan to address this issue might look like the following:

Inform Other Departments

Contact John from Sales and tell him we will be sending weekly updates on complete inventory.

Hold interdepartmental meetings monthly so that all are informed and also have the opportunity to ask questions.

Inform upper management of all steps to be taken.

Notify human resources.

Communicate technical problems in general to all and in particular to those who need to deal with them directly.

Create better working relationships by greater communication and courteous interactions.

If personal conflicts arise, deal with them quickly instead of allowing them to fester and infect everyone.

By having meetings and initiating weekly updates, information will be over-shared to enhance productivity.

Follow up and let all involved know what action is to be taken. Implement by writing and discussing decisions, actions, responsibilities, and dates.

6. *Plan outcomes.* Answer this question: What needs to be maintained, acquired, eliminated, avoided? Measure/compare this with the planning outcomes (best/worst). Consider the best and worst outcomes to explore possibilities.

7. *Reassess and follow up.* Ask: What has been accomplished? What has changed? What is different? What action needs to be taken now? What follow-up effort/action needs to be taken in the future?

By working through the models and steps presented in this section, you can identify the problem and come to a well-thought-out, creative solution.

RESOURCES

Morgan, G. (1997). *Imaginization.* San Francisco, CA: Berrett-Koehler.

Nonaka, I., & Takeuchi, H. (1995). *How Japanese companies foster creativity and innovation for competitive advantage.* New York: Oxford University Press.

What Methods Can I Use to Generate Solutions for Problems?

IN THIS CHAPTER, we will cover two different techniques for generating solutions to problems: brainstorming and the fishbone diagram.

Brainstorming

When brainstorming, it is important to generate as many ideas as possible, using one idea as a take-off point for generating more ideas, clarifying items to expand the thinking about the original idea or problem. Studies have shown that some of the best ideas come late in the brainstorming process. Brainstorming is based on two assumptions:

1. Suspending judgment about an idea increases productivity and promotes the generation of ideas.

2. Because so many and varied ideas are generated, quantity promotes quality, that is, quality ideas can be chosen from the quantity of ideas.

Effective brainstorming builds a sense of trust, openness, honesty, and respect within a group and a willingness to accept, listen, and share ideas. It also supports efforts to achieve specific goals. In order to brainstorm effectively, set some ground rules and obtain group consensus on them. Your ground rules should include the following:

- We will post the specific goal for the brainstorming session and ideas should relate to it.
- All ideas will be written on a flip chart.
- ALL ideas will be acknowledged (one obscure idea may eventually generate a solution).
- No criticism of any idea will be allowed.
- Every person at the session is asked to contribute at least one idea.
- We'll emphasize quantity over quality.
- Two people will take notes so that no ideas are lost.
- There are no time constraints, as they tend to inhibit creative thinking.

Leading a Brainstorming Session

A brainstorming session must be focused on the goal. Its purpose should be to fulfill specific business expectations or address specific problems. Both immediate and long-term responses should be developed through the combined energies and personalities brought together.

A brainstorming session has three basic functions:

1. To identify and specifically address a business issue.
2. To create a forum in which viewpoints are exchanged constructively and safely.
3. To establish a plan of action and a short- or long-term timetable.

The meeting leader is responsible for keeping a brainstorming session focused and promoting discussion on the expected results and for delegating follow-up action. The leader should keep the following points in mind when conducting any brainstorming session:

Effective Brainstorming Begins with Planning. The leader organizes the agenda, secures the participants, and determines the length of the meeting ahead of time to ensure that all issues are discussed. So that participants do not feel pressured by time, it should be made known that an additional meeting can be scheduled if enough information is not generated at the first session.

The Leader Keeps the Group Focused. This does not mean that the leader is the only one who talks. In fact, the leader ensures that everyone has a chance to speak. The leader also revises the agenda during the meeting if discussions run too long.

Conflict Is Common During a Brainstorming Session. An open, honest exchange of ideas can often generate creative solutions. When conflict arises, the leader paraphrases the issues and then draws all members into a productive sharing of ideas while acknowledging resistance among the members.

Follow-Up Is Essential. As part of any brainstorming session there must be follow-up. A copy of the meeting minutes should be sent to everyone, along with a list of actions to be taken and by whom.

Fishbone Diagrams

The fishbone diagram (sometimes called a cause/effect diagram) allows the team to explore the reasons for an outcome. Graphically, the team identifies possible causes related to a problem. The fishbone diagram is used for the following:

- To identify and focus on a problem;
- To collect a great deal of information about the problem; and,
- To focus on a major category or cause/effect in relationship to the problem.

To set up a fishbone diagram, use these steps:

1. Identify the problem.
2. Obtain agreement that this is the problem and write it on the main horizontal line.

3. Add "bones" to represent categories or causes of the problem and write the names on sticky notes placed so that they come off from the "backbone."

4. Categorize and explore reasons to support why the problem exists, and move the sticky bones to the proper categories.

5. Now write the causes directly onto the bones in the proper categories for discussion.

Some Sample Categories

People	Materials	Equipment
Time	Services	Changes
Methods	Travel	Policies
Procedures	Places	Costs

See the following example of a fishbone diagram.

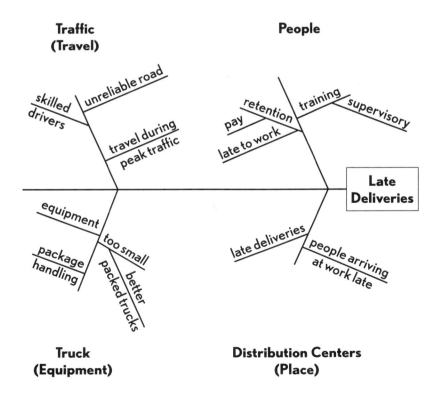

This example shows the problem that was identified (late deliveries) and the possible causes for the late deliveries. The diagram lists possible causes for the late deliveries in categories so each can be explored and resolved separately. To narrow down the possibilities, many facilitators ask "why" four times about each item. A fishbone diagram can be used in conjunction with the seven-step creative problem-solving model (covered earlier in this part of the book (p. 232).

By looking at problems before they become crises, you can better resolve them. When dealing with problems, recognize and use your own strengths, assess the risks of a change, collect information, and have the courage to begin solving the problem.

RESOURCES

Brassard, M., & Ritter, D. (1994). *The memory jogger II*. Methuen, MA: Goal/GQC.

Gatto, R. (1992). *Teamwork through flexible leadership*. Pittsburgh, PA: GTA Press.

Gibson, J., Ivancevich, J., & Donnelly, J. (1997). *Organizations: Behavior, structure, processes*. Boston, MA: Irwin/McGraw-Hill.

Kanter, R.M., Kao, J., & Wiersma, F. (1997). *Innovation*. New York: Harper Business.

Knowles, M., & Knowles, H. (1972). *Introduction to group dynamics*. Upper Saddle River, NJ: Prentice Hall.

Michalko, M. (1991). *Thinkertoys*. Berkeley, CA: Ten Speed Press.

Osborn, A.F. (1963). *Applied imagination* (3rd rev. ed.). New York: Scribner.

Résumé Writing

Q How Can I Create an Effective Résumé?

AT SOME TIME IN YOUR CAREER, you may be faced with the need to change jobs, whether because of downsizing, mergers, or desire on your part for a change. An important tool in this process is the résumé. Writing an informative, attractive, and compelling résumé is possible if you follow these simple guidelines.

- Remember that there is no perfect way to write a résumé.

- Your approach should highlight your strengths and answer the questions you assume an interviewer would ask and give reasons for him or her calling you in for an interview.

- Your résumé should show why you are unique.

- Your résumé should stand out. Be creative, but not artsy. Elegant format and design are better than lots of splashy fonts and graphics (which you won't have room for anyway).

- Keep it short.
- Include your objective for working in the industry/field. You could note that you want to use your work experience or education or that you want to develop to your fullest potential.
- Organize your information under these headings:
  - *Objective.* List the specific area in which you would like to work. You should make several different résumés mirroring the area of the job for which you are applying.
  - *Professional Experience/Work-Related Experience.* Note skills that can be transferred from job to job.
  - *Significant Experience.* Life experiences, organizational awards, professional associations, volunteer experiences.
  - *Areas of Strength.* Leadership, special skills, teamwork, project management, and so forth.
  - *Computer Experience.* List programs used and degree of experience.
  - *Academic Experience.* Academic courses, certificates, and achievements related to job.
- List information beginning with the most recent and working backward.
- Do not include health or marital status.
- Your cover letter should be brief and to the point.
- Have a friend read your résumé for flow and spelling.

Remember that interviewers see many résumés. Make sure yours is the one the interviewer wants to naturally pick out of the stack.

Sample Résumé

Wan A. Job

777 Main Street
Anytown, Anystate, USA
(111) 222-3333

Objective To work within the investment banking industry utilizing my experience as a banker and manager.

Professional Experience

1989–2000 USA Bank
Responsible for developing and managing the investment department; establishing a mutual fund portfolio; and managing a profitable department of ten people

1980–1989 North South Bank
Responsible for commercial loans. Worked within the regional community supporting local business

Academic Experience B.S. in Business, ABC University
MBA, XYZ University
Honors—Magna Cum Laude

Personal Experience Volunteer, Boy Scouts of America
Board Member, Now Corporation
Sunday School Teacher

Areas of Strength

Leadership	Business Knowledge
Strategic Thinking	Management
Teamwork	Commitment
Communication	Writing

Computer Experience Microsoft Word
WordPerfect
Excel

Professional Organizations American Society for Bankers
American Brokers' Association

Sample Cover Letter

Write a cover letter to accompany your résumé. Be brief.

Dear Sir/Madam:

[State your purpose]	I am interested in the position of . . . . Enclosed please find a copy of my résumé.
[When/where to reach you]	I can be reached at . . . during the hours of . . . or at . . . between. . . .
[State objectives and emphasize skills]	I would like to be a member of your company because I could. . . .
[Close]	I look forward to discussing with you my ability to fulfill the position of. . . .

Sincerely,

[Your Signature]	*Wan A. Job*
[Your Typed Name]	Wan. A. Job
[Enclose your résumé]	Enclosure: Résumé

RESOURCES

Asher, D., & Asher, D. (1999). *The overnight resume.* Berkeley, CA: Ten Speed Press.

Bolles, R.N. (1999). *What color is your parachute?* Berkeley, CA: Ten Speed Press.

Parker, Y. *The damn good resume guide* (3rd ed.). Berkeley, CA: Ten Speed Press.

Retention and Termination

How Can I Retain Employees?

THE BEST WAY to retain employees is to find out what they can achieve, ask them how they plan to achieve it, and then let them go to work—assuming they want something that's for the good of the organization. Retention of employees creates a stable work environment. A stable environment and workforce establish working relationships with internal and external customers and demonstrate high performance. Retention planning for an employee needs to begin the first day of his or her employment. Employees want to feel involved, a part of the organization. They also need to know what is available in terms of career development. If possible, an experienced employee should be available for the new employee to talk with. This is an informal way to help to socialize the new employee to the organization.

Creating an Environment for Employee Retention

Mission Statement

The process of keeping employees begins with a clear understanding of your organization. Clarity about the services your organization provides and the type of clients you want to attract and hold provide an understanding of your organization for employees. If there's not a fit with their own personal goals and mission, they're unlikely to stay.

Orientation

The orientation process influences work and productivity. Hiring and orientation processes should include introduction of new employees to people and clients, an employee handbook, copies of the organizational mission, assignment of a specific mentor, a discussion of career potential, clear expectations for how you want the person to work with clients and to work internally, and a discussion of how the person can be successful in the organization.

Leadership/Followership

Leadership style should be such that it creates, articulates, and translates day-to-day employee actions into ways to meet organizational goals. The managers' leadership style needs to be chosen consciously, not just "This is the way I do it."

Communication

Communication, both formal and informal, is the lifeline of the organization. Formal lines of communication are established by managers. Informal communication is the gossip line. Formal lines of communication need to be stronger than the informal lines.

Career Path

From day one it should be clear to each employee in the organization the opportunities that are available. It should also be made clear how to take advantage of these opportunities. The organizational structure, culture, and reward system should reflect the type of talent and skills that the organization wants. Projecting a professional image, meeting client expectations for performance, and upcoming organizational expansion and development need to be discussed, as appropriate.

The Right People

Try to think long-term rather than short-term when hiring people. What are the qualifications you will need in years to come? Outline the skills that are most important now and for future development.

Selection

You must understand the type of competencies you have now and those you need and want. Be aware of what type of people your organization actually needs and whether the people you have already fit the type of organization you want to become. Decide on the type of people you want to add to the mix to create the organization you want. Ask questions; look for actions more than words to evaluate people's specific skills, client relationships, creativity, communication skills, and teamwork.

The Hiring Process

Employee retention begins with the hiring process. It continues by providing the employee a good orientation, good leadership, open communication across the organization, and clear expectations of job performance. The hiring process must include a discussion of why the person was hired, expectations of job performance, how the person will fit into the organization, who will mentor the person, and the person's strengths and areas for development.

By continuing this process, the result can be a stable, experienced workforce, which is the backbone of any organization.

RESOURCES

Ambrose, L. (1998). *A mentor's companion.* Chicago, IL: Perrone-Ambrose.

Schuler, H., Farr, J.L., & Smith, M. (1993). *Personnel selection and assessment: Individual and organizational perspectives.* Hillsdale, NJ: Lawrence Erlbaum.

QHow Should I Handle Termination of an Employee?

SOMETIMES AN EMPLOYEE must be terminated, for any number of reasons. Some of the most common are listed below.

- The employee does not fulfill job responsibilities and presently does not have the skill set nor interest in performing them.

- A reduction in force is necessary because of management decisions not based on employee ability.

- The employee willfully abuses or breaks an organizational policy, for example, continually comes late to work, displays insubordination, or verbally or physically abuses another employee.

Disciplining employees is another very difficult task that managers may need to perform. The point of discipline is to correct a problem. However, willful disobedience after chances for correction have been given leads to termination.

Contributing factors include the severity of the infraction, how similar problems have been handled, and the level or position of the employee.

Also, every manager will probably have an employee at some time who was hired for a position for which he or she is unable to fulfill the responsibilities.

It is important to give any employee facing termination a chance to alter behavior and/or develop the skills needed to fulfill the job responsibilities. However, once it becomes clear that the employee does not have the skill base or will not be capable of fulfilling the job responsibilities, it is better to terminate the person. Most organizations have policies and procedures that need to be followed. It is up to you as the manager to explain to the employee why he or she is being terminated.

Review the list below to focus on what is appropriate in your situation to help you terminate an employee and to help lower the stress for the employee.

- Make sure the employee receives performance feedback indicating why he or she is being discharged.

- Support the employee. Don't let him or her feel like a failure. Focus on what he or she learned from the job.

- Ask the employee to write his or her thoughts on paper. This can be helpful to focus the person's thoughts.

- Many discharges can happen because the right person was in the wrong job; let the employee know if this was the case.

- If termination is due to downsizing:
  - Help the employee understand the company policy on layoffs and relocations.
  - Support the employee. Use facts to disarm any negative emotions.
  - Help the employee to have confidence in him- or herself to succeed in the future.
  - Let the employee know that other employees will respond positively to someone with a positive attitude.

Steps to Termination

Before terminating any employee, have documentation of events that led up to the decision. It is imperative that you, as a manager, keep a log on each employee, listing all infractions and incidents, coupled with your response in each case, such as verbal reprimands, letters of reprimand, and at least two warnings, both verbal and written, telling the employee that his or her infractions may lead to termination. Review all of your documentation with that person. It is usually best to have an employee sign a warning letter so there is no discussion later about whether or not you discussed the issue together.

Make sure you have the following information in hand:

- Your company's policy on termination (from your HR department);

- Reason for termination (backed up by documentation);

- When employee will be told of termination (usually late on a Friday to avoid disruption in the workplace);

- Specific date of termination (if not immediate);

- Benefits due employee (vacation time, duration of health insurance, retirement funds, etc.);

- Who will inform the employee (usually the manager and an HR representative);

- Whether the employee will be allowed to resign rather than be fired; and

- A termination form for the employee to sign.

Having all of the above information available will protect you, your company, and the terminated employee.

The following is a example of a termination for cause.

Joe, an inside salesperson, comes in late for work two or three times a week. He is to start at 8:30 a.m. and work until 4:30 p.m., with a scheduled lunch break. He has been coming in at 8:45 or 9:00. Josette, the manager of the inside sales force, has spoken with Joe on two occasions when he was late. He said he was tired and missed the bus. Joe said he would come in on time thereafter. Joe has never made an effort to make up the missed work and continues to be the first to leave at 4:30.

Two weeks go by, and Joe comes in at 8:50 one morning without saying anything to Josette. She calls Joe into her office and asks why he is late, stating that he knows that the work day begins at 8:30 and it is important for customer service. Joe says it isn't his fault, that traffic was heavy and the bus was late. Josette writes a disciplinary correction letter and has Joe sign the letter, stating that he will not be late for work again.

Three weeks pass, and Joe comes in late on two consecutive mornings. Josette realizes that Joe's being habitually late has started to affect the morale of the other inside salespeople. Josette calls Joe in, reviews his file with him, and tells him he is being terminated for disciplinary reasons.

Involuntary termination, although never pleasant, must be done when an employee ignores or breaks the stated work rules. Justly enforcing involuntary termination for an uncooperative employee can maintain morale among other employees and uphold organizational policy.

RESOURCES

Fournies, F. (1987). *Coaching for improved work performance*. New York: McGraw-Hill.

Gatto, R. (1999). *Personal mentoring guide*. Unpublished manuscript. Gatto Training Associates, 733 Washington Road, Pittsburgh, PA 15228.

Gibson, J., Ivancevich, J., & Donnelly, J. (1997). *Organizations: Behavior, structure, processes*. Boston, MA: Irwin/McGraw-Hill.

Ludden, L., & Capozzoli, T. (2000). *Supervisor savvy*. Indianapolis, IN: JIST Works.

Ragins, B.R., & Cotton, J.L. (1999). Mentor functions and outcomes: A comparison of men and women in formal and informal mentoring relationships. *Journal of Applied Psychology, 84*(4), 529–550.

Tobias, P.H., & Sauter, S. (1997). *Job rights and survival strategies: A handbook for terminated employees*. Cincinnati, OH: National Employee Rights Institute.

Selling

How Can I Improve My Sales Techniques?

MORE BUSINESSES THAN EVER are selling products and services through more venues than ever: over the Internet, through direct mail, over the phone, through warehouse clubs, and on and on. It is important to develop a competitive edge to be successful. To improve your sales techniques, consider the following points:

- Selling is like doctoring. Diagnose first: Who are my customers and what is my strategy for selling to them? Prescribe second: What is my goal? The art of selling is helping the customer/client make an informed choice.

- Know your customers. Know what their companies want; know what their companies do not want; know the company's problems; know who in the company has the buying power.

- Know your competition. Know what the competition is offering.

- Emphasize what *you* can do for the customer, not what the competition cannot do.

- Actions speak louder than words. If you say you will do it, do it!

- Service your customer beyond the expected. It is well worth the effort and may pay future benefits.

- Never think of a sales call as wasted. By your building rapport and a history, that customer may come to you in the future.

- Help the customer make an informed decision and think through the decision-making process for buying your product or service. Present everything you can offer.

- Ask the customer questions; ask the customer's opinion. Listen. Record everything. According to John Graham, president of Graham Communications, the chances of making a sale increase the longer the customer talks (Paterson, 1999).

- Follow up. Make sure your customer is satisfied. If not, find out what you can to do make the customer satisfied. Follow up and follow through.

Preparation

Preparation is key to a successful sales call. Not only should you know your company and its products, but you should also know the potential customer's company well. Answer these questions:

- Who is my customer?
- Who is my competition?
- What do I know about the customer's company?
- Are there any traits I should be aware of?

- What do I want to achieve at this meeting? Is the purpose to introduce myself, establish rapport, or make the sale?

When you're planning a sales call, also keep in mind the following reasons why sales calls sometimes end with no sale:

- No relationship established;
- Customer need was not met;
- Poor interaction; seller didn't listen to customer;
- Poor sales technique: too much talking and not enough listening;
- Wrong product, location, image, or service;
- Wrong price-for-value relationship;
- Wrong timing; or
- Customer wasn't involved.

All of the above can be avoided by doing your "homework"—by being prepared.

Charting the Process

Chart your sales approach to help you see all the steps in the process. The following chart is a look at all the steps a customer goes through in search of a product or service. Following this chart, you can see that a customer is made aware of the product/service through a marketing effort. The customer then makes an inquiry, which can be directed to the salesperson. An appointment is set, the salesperson meets the customer, finds any customer needs or desired actions, finds a way to meet those needs, makes the sale, and follows up to ensure that the customer is satisfied. After payment is received, the salesperson adds the customer to the customer file and calls periodically to see whether the customer has additional needs. This becomes the marketing effort, and the process begins again.

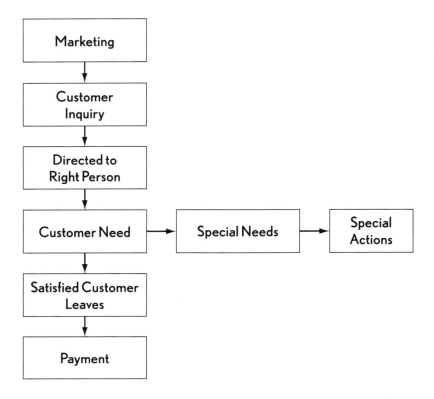

To change your selling techniques to improve your sales goals, try the following:

1. Draw a flow chart that identifies your *current* process.

2. Draw a new flow chart featuring the process steps that *should* occur.

3. Compare the two charts. Is there a step that is not on your current process? Identify problems in your process and then find ways to enhance that process for better sales and service.

RESOURCES

Chapman, E. (1992). *Sales training basics: A primer for those new to selling* (3rd ed.). Menlo Park, CA: Crisp.

Paterson, J. (1999). The evolution of a sales strategy. In Bell Atlantic's *Smart Business Update, 6*(3).

Sexual Harassment

Q What Should I Know About Sexual Harassment?

SEXUAL HARASSMENT is defined by the Equal Employment Opportunity Commission (EEOC) as follows: "Unwelcome sexual advances, requests for sexual favors, and other verbal or physical conduct of a sexual nature constitutes sexual harassment when submission to or rejection of this conduct explicitly or implicitly affects an individual's employment, unreasonably interferes with an individual's work performance, or creates an intimidating, hostile, or offensive work environment."

This definition does not specifically identify what constitutes harassment, but several factors should be kept in mind when determining whether certain actions might be viewed as harassment. These factors are listed below:

- The frequency of the discrimination/harassment;
- The severity of the discrimination/harassment;
- Whether the discrimination/harassment is physically threatening or humiliating; and

- Whether the discrimination/harassment unreasonably interferes with job performance.

Steps to Lower Liability

There are several pre-emptory steps that employers can take in regard to sexual harassment. These have proven to be helpful to other companies.

Written Policy

Have a written policy in place concerning harassment. All employees should be provided with the company's written policy on discrimination and harassment. Such a policy should contain the following:

- Encouragement to employees to report incidents;
- What constitutes discrimination and/or harassment per government guidelines;
- Steps to be taken to file a complaint within the company;
- How the employer will respond to complaints it receives;
- Steps the employer will take to investigate; and
- How the results of the investigation will be communicated to the employee who complains.

Immediate Response

Respond to all complaints received. The courts have held employers responsible simply because they "knew, or *should have known*" about complaints and did not respond to them (*Personnel Policy Manual,* 1999).

It is imperative that all organizations have an internal complaint process that employees are aware of and that employers follow through on any complaints received. The process for filing and responding to complaints should contain all of following points:

- The complainant should first file a written statement to the appropriate person in the organization, as outlined in the company's written policy.

- The complainant should be assured of confidentiality and a promise of non-retaliation.

- The appropriate personnel should investigate the complaint and respond to the complainant within a *reasonable* amount of time.

- The results of the investigation should be documented and communicated to all parties involved.

- If appropriate, the organization should discipline the offending party according to its written policy.

Educated Workforce

Companies must take a commonsense approach to avoiding sexual harassment in the first place. There are several ways to lessen the risk of sexual harassment incidents. By educating employees, you enhance their awareness and put them on notice that harassment will not be tolerated in the workplace. Here are some ideas:

- Have all employees attend a training workshop to educate them on what constitutes sexual harassment and how to avoid it.

- Institute some sensitivity training so that people are more attuned to others' feelings.

- Use humor as a release of tension as long as it is appropriate and is not offensive.

- Treat everyone with dignity and respect, which sets the tone for others.

- If there is any doubt as to whether an action, statement, joke, or response is inappropriate, remind employees *not* to do it or say it.

Having clear policies in place helps both the employer and the employee create a non-hostile workplace. It also shows that you, the employer, have taken action to try to prevent harassment and appropriately deal with it if it occurs. The bottom line is that harassment lawsuits are expensive to defend. The best defense is prevention.

RESOURCES

Kirshenberg, S. (1999, September). Sexual harassment. *Training & Development,* pp. 29–32.

Personal Policy Service, Inc. (1998). *A service for management: Sexual harassment.* Louisville, KY: Author.

Personnel Policy Services, Inc. (1999). *EEOC guidelines.* www.ppspublishers.com.

Personnel Policy Services, Inc. (1999). *HRMatters.* www.ppspublishers.com.

Personnel Policy Service, Inc. (1999). *Personnel policy manual.* www.ppspublishers.com.

Pierce, E., Smolinski, C.A., & Rosen, B. (1998). Why sexual harassment complaints fall on deaf ears. *Academy of Management Executive, 12,* 41–54.

Steingold, F. (1998). *The employer's legal handbook.* Berkeley, CA: Nolo Press.

Stress Management

How Can I Manage Stress?

STRESS IS UNIVERSAL. All people are affected by it in varying degrees. Only the causes and how people deal with stress are different. Stress is becoming ever more of a problem because of modern workplace pressures. Your goal is to control stress so it does not control you.

Think of a violin string. There needs to be a certain level of tension on the string so that it can make music. If the string has no tension, it will not create a musical sound. If it has too much tension, it can snap. Stress from life events creates the tension; people are the string and wood of the violin. People have different levels of stress and abilities to work within and tolerate it. Just like the violin string, we can snap. Some of the events that cause stress are:

- Marriage or divorce,
- Illness or death in the family,
- Financial problems,
- Change of any sort, such as moving or taking a new job,

- Workload increasing or decreasing,
- Constant deadlines,
- Lack of support, and
- Continual conflict.

Some of the effects of stress include:

- Tight neck muscles,
- Churning stomach,
- Increased blood pressure,
- Headaches,
- Ulcers,
- Clenching the jaw,
- Anxiety, and
- Increased alcohol or tobacco use.

Before managing your stress, you need to determine what is at the root of it. The following steps will help you in managing your stress:

1. Identify causes for your stress, for example, time, family, money, work-related conflicts, too many demands, or self-doubt.

2. Identify how stress manifests itself for you. What are the signs of your stress, for example, having a short temper, not finishing projects, feeling overwhelmed, being angry, blaming others, or withdrawing.

3. Find ways to lessen stress, such as voicing what you have not expressed, discussing your stress with a friend, or writing out the causes. Reread the causes you have written, underline important issues, and develop an action plan to deal with each cause.

4. Instead of worrying about actions that you may already have taken or statements you have made in anger, work out a best/worst case scenario for controlling your next stressful incident. After you describe a

worst case scenario, figure out how you want to deal with it if it were to happen. A best case may be the outcome you desire. Look at the model below, which shows three items: what was said, what the causes were, and what the best/worst outcomes would be. Planning for stress in this way can help you to deal with it more easily.

Statement	Causes	Outcomes (Best/Worst)
Said I would never work with her again!	I was angry about the meeting with Mary this morning.	She is really upset with me; we will have a difficult time working together (worst); I will talk to Mary and we will discuss it and improve our working relationship (best).

5. Prioritize. Begin each day by writing a realistic "to-do" list; at the end of each day write an "I did" list, showing all you accomplished that day. Give yourself credit for accomplishments. The purpose of the to-do list is to create a focus. A problem arises when you put too much in your to-do list and are then unable to complete it. Keep the list reasonable. See it as a tool, not a challenge. Seeing what you actually accomplished on the "I did" list can relieve stress.

6. Be honest with yourself. Don't try to accomplish more than what is possible in any given period of time.

7. Take at least fifteen minutes of uninterrupted time for yourself daily. Leave your immediate work area and take a brief walk outside or have an informal discussion with a co-worker. These activities can relax you and even enhance your productivity.

8. Leave your immediate work environment for lunch. Do not eat at your desk. The point of lunch is to recharge and refresh yourself.

9. Find an approach that relieves your stress. Take a walk, read, do deep breathing exercises, or listen to music.

10. You can control stress instead of letting it control you by controlling your thoughts and attitudes toward situations and people.

Definitions of Stressors

Although stress is universal, the causes of stress vary from person to person. Something that is stressful for one person may be a source of relaxation for another. Identify what causes you stress and determine whether that stress is helpful (*eustress*) or harmful (*distress*).

Eustress

Good stress is an uplifting feeling or anxiousness before a special occasion (such as a speaking engagement). Athletes call this "getting psyched." Eustress is usually related to a special event.

Distress

Distress is a persistent condition that negatively affects you physically (rapid breathing and pulse, high blood pressure); mentally (anxiety, tension); and behaviorally (short-tempered, irrational). It is characterized by heavy workload, not being able to complete a job to your satisfaction, performing tasks you do not like, operating under severe time constraints, feeling stuck in a particular job, or working for an unappreciative boss. The entire work environment can become stressful when you feel stuck.

Stress or anxiety precludes your being able to learn new things and can alter your behavior or ability to perform. If you are tense or anxious, you will demonstrate that by your actions. But, as we showed above, if you take the time to analyze the cause of stress, you will be able to respond to it more appropriately. In other words, if you become nervous or upset around a particular person or in a particular situation, you can develop a strategy to deal with the cause. Think about areas in which you have been strong and successful: "I completed that project ahead of schedule and saved the company a lot of money. I am a successful person." Think about yourself as in control and don't dwell on inadequacies. Remind yourself that this particular person or situation does not have control over you and that you can control your own feelings. If feasible, you can also plan to avoid the person or situation as much as possible. The more you are aware of your causes of stress, the more you can rid yourself of stress in the future.

Three C's for Lowering Stress

Commitment, control, and challenge are three important factors for learning to combat stress. The three C's provide a way to structure your thoughts when you're under stress: (1) *committing* yourself toward something you value, (2) *controlling* yourself and therefore the situation, and (3) *challenging* yourself through learning to handle stressful situations. Use the model in this way.

Commitment

Decide what you are committed to achieve. This can help you to focus. The more you are committed, the more you control a situation. What are you committed to accomplish? What values are you committed to fulfill and fight for? What is the purpose and meaning of what you want to accomplish? There is great value in deciding what you stand for and fighting for it. Maslow (1970) called these "being values." Commitment brings culture, intellect, desire, opportunity, and achievement together. Being aware of what is really important to you can allow you to realize what is not worth being stressed about.

Control

Do you have a sense of control or do you feel that someone or a situation is controlling you? Are you an influencer or decision maker in your own life's work? Have you accepted yourself and given yourself due credit? Strive to find meaning in your life. Being in control of yourself lessens anxiety and stress.

Challenge

Do you challenge yourself to reach your potential and use all your gifts and talents? Do you feel accomplished and fulfilled by utilizing your abilities? Or do you feel overwhelmed when challenged? If you are facing a challenge, review the skills and knowledge you already have to deal with the problem. By being realistic and accepting challenges as opportunities, you can relax and dissipate stressors.

The case study that follows features an employee named Bill. As you read about Bill, think about the concepts presented in this section. Use what you have learned about controlling stress and try to apply it to Bill's situation. It will help you to refine and focus your own thoughts about dealing with stress. Look for causes of stress in Bill's life. After you have finished, consider what you would say to Bill if he were a friend of yours. Finally, if you were objectively counseling Bill, what would you advise him to do?

Case Study

Bill is in his mid-forties. He is a middle manager in the Manufacturing Division of a large chemical corporation. Everyone in the office seems to get along with him. Bill knows the twenty employees he manages, their spouses, and most of their children. On Mondays, he talks about football and generally creates a relaxed atmosphere in the office. By all outward appearances, Bill is cool, calm, and relaxed.

Bill was promoted five years ago from the Research and Development Department to the Manufacturing Division. His main responsibility is to understand the needs of the customer and what the competition is developing. Then he updates senior executives as to market and competitive trends. He is the link between the customer and the corporation. He continually feels that he is fighting the clock. Bill realizes he tries to do too much, but thinks, "I'll try to do it anyway."

Almost every morning he rushes to work early to get a jump on completing his work. Sometimes on his way to work he runs yellow lights because he is anxious to get to the job. It seems as though he is always fighting fires and managing crises. Last week a worker was injured by spilled chemicals, and Bill had to call the employee's wife and file all of the necessary medical forms. He then had to explain to the group vice president why the division's safety record is so poor. He simply said, "We are under a lot of pressure to produce."

Phone calls continually interrupt Bill's work day, and he attends a lot of meetings. Often it takes him half a day just to return phone calls and even longer to actually reach the person whose call he is returning. He leaves so many voice mail messages that he forgets whom he called and why. He wants to delegate more responsibilities to others, but thinks that he can do the work more efficiently; he believes that he knows best what the executives and customers want and need.

Bill is getting to work earlier and leaving later to try to get the job done. He knows he should exercise but does not have time. It seems that he goes to work and lives on coffee and cigarettes. He does, however, usually manage to have lunch.

Bill's two boys play on high school sports teams, and he often misses their games because he is at work or traveling. His wife says she understands that he is under a lot of pressure, but would like him to be at home more. Bill feels caught between two worlds—neither of which is going well. He likes his job and receives a fair salary, but the tradeoffs are consuming his life. He lives in an affluent area with an excellent school system. Both of the boys will be in college in less than four years. To quit his job for one with less pressure is out of the question. He wonders, "Who would take a scientist in his mid-forties with an MBA and pay the same salary?"

Sometimes, when Bill is at his desk, his neck feels as though it has knots in it. Last week Bill felt a tightness in his chest while in a meeting. He started to become warm and perspire. He thought, "I have to relax. I'll be all right. I just have to take deep breaths and lay off the cigarettes." Bill knows he will only have to do this a few more years until the division gets on its feet and meets all the quotas. Bill says, "I can handle it awhile longer." Sometimes Bill wishes he could forget the entire job and go fishing.

What advice would you give Bill? Consider your advice under these topic headings:

- Ways to lessen Bill's job-related distress;
- Bill's health needs;
- Bill's family needs;
- Bill's thoughts about himself;
- Time management;
- Leadership (people-orientation versus task-orientation); and
- Management style.

Obviously, one thing Bill could do would be to express his thoughts. It's not enough to ponder and mentally contemplate an action plan. Distressful ideas should be put on paper and analyzed. Words written on paper usually are analyzed and interpreted differently from spoken words. Writing ideas is not a panacea, but it is a good way to focus.

How do you know whether you have stress? The signs for stress begin with a high feeling of frustration. Some additional signs of stress include the following:

- Low self-esteem,
- Irritability,
- Problems sleeping,
- Lack of focus,
- Feeling unhappy,
- Worrying, and
- Weight change.

These signs can be warning signals that you have high levels of stress.

RESOURCES

Holmes, T.H., & Rahe, R.H. (1967). Social readjustment rating scale. *Journal of Psychosomatic Research, 11,* 213–218.

Maslow, A. (1970). *Motivation and personality* (2nd ed.). New York: Harper and Row.

Quick, J.C., Murphy, L.R., & Hurrell, J.J., Jr. (1992). *Stress and well-being at work.* Washington, DC: American Psychological Association.

Selye, H. (Ed.). (1980). *Selye's guide to stress research* (Vol. 1). New York: Van Nostrand Reinhold.

Supervisory Skills

Q What Skills and Knowledge Do I Require as a Supervisor?

SUPERVISORS ARE the link between management and associates or direct reports. Effective supervisors lead others, establish goals, and help to support the corporate culture. When a supervisor successfully communicates the organization's expectations, direct reports understand what they have to do, comply with requests and expectations, and, ultimately, fulfill their roles.

Successful supervisors should:

- Know the jobs direct reports perform. The supervisor can best work with a direct report by knowing the level of job performance needed to fulfill the job.

- Develop ownership for a work area or process. Ownership is a powerful way of demonstrating commitment and going beyond job tasks. Ownership is demonstrated through a complete fulfillment of supervisory responsibilities.

- Effectively communicate goals and objectives. A supervisor must be an effective communicator. A good way to communicate with direct reports is to hold frequent, brief meetings on what went right, what needs to be corrected, and what needs to be done next.

- Listen effectively. A key to supervision is effective listening, both to management and to direct reports. Supervisors must translate what management wants to those who will do it.

- Treat employees respectfully, honestly, and openly. Treating people with respect is a basic tenet in the workplace. Treating employees like adults gives them the opportunity to think and act in a mature way. Employees relate to a supervisor who demonstrates open, honest, and respectful skills, even during disagreements.

- Be able to supervise a diverse, multicultural workforce. The supervisor must adapt his or her style so that employees will understand what is expected. Being flexible addresses the needs of the employees.

- Explain what is expected and continually update employees. The more clearly the supervisor presents his or her expectations of the level of achievement, the less often the work will need to be redone.

- Support employees in their efforts to succeed on the job. Once expectations are clear, ask the employees how they will fulfill the job. Ask what they think is required, what they might do differently, and what alternatives there might be.

- Have integrity and build trust. These two hold the supervisor-employee relationship together so that the employee is willing to act on what a supervisor says.

- Recognize excellent performance. Recognition is a great way to motivate employees and encourage them to put forth maximum effort. "Catch an employee doing something right" should be the watchword.

- Promote teamwork. Teamwork is essential for effectively and efficiently completing the work. Effective supervisors coach individuals and create teams.

- Set a good example by modeling standards of conduct and performance. The actions that you take as a supervisor communicate far more loudly than words alone.

- Evaluate employees fairly. Equity among employees is essential. Outstanding work should be recognized, and no favoritism should be shown.

- Schedule vacations, breaks, and work assignments. Supervisors have to be organized administrators with an established process for planning employee vacations and breaks and for distributing the workload.

- Reprimand, discipline, and deal fairly with all associates. Discipline is a tool for corrective action. It is important to ensure that all employees understand when they do something right and when they need to change. The point of reprimand is to alter employee behavior. A supervisor should focus on the behavior or the issue, not on the person.

- Maintain a working environment that is safe, both physically and mentally. Emotional safety and comfort are important for reaching a high level of productivity.

- Resolve conflicts effectively. To resolve conflict, the effective supervisor must focus on agreement, not on disagreement, starting with the area of agreement, rather than the issue or conflict.

- Be able to interview and hire new associates. The effective supervisor uses good interview questions to identify what a person can do and whether the person works well with others. He or she takes the time to interview fully to avoid having to fill the position again in the near future.

- Give appropriate feedback to encourage employee development. Feedback is the supervisor's tool for employee development. As a supervisor develops employees, the supervisor also develops him- or herself.

- Collect associates' suggestions and, when appropriate, implement them. Involvement is a key to building a team and motivating employees. The people who do the work should be asked for their suggestions to enhance, alter, or develop alternatives for the work. A supervisor who can implement employee suggestions demonstrates a participatory team approach.

- Ensure that direct reports follow appropriate rules and regulations. The supervisor establishes clear and fair rules and regulations. The simpler the rules are to understand and the stronger the commitment is to hold employees accountable to those rules, the better the supervisor.

- Encourage continuous improvement in processes. Supervisors encourage through open dialogue. This challenges employees and continues to motivate them. Supervisors walk around the work site to let employees know they are interested in the process and what is happening.

- Develop employees through mentoring and coaching. Mentoring and coaching are one-on-one development processes. Supervisors observe, ask why the employees do what they do, and give feedback. They set an open, communicative atmosphere, ask the employees for their thoughts, and recognize effort.

RESOURCES

Gibson, J., Ivancevich, J., & Donnelly, J. (1997). *Organizations.* Boston, MA: Irwin/McGraw-Hill.

Greenberg, J. (1999). *Managing behavior in organizations.* Upper Saddle River, NJ: Prentice Hall.

Humphrey, B., & Stokes, J. (1999). *The 21st century supervisor: Nine essential skills for frontline leaders.* San Francisco, CA: Jossey-Bass/Pfeiffer.

Mager, R., & Pipe, P. (1984). *Analyzing performance problems.* Belmont, CA: Lake.

Teams

How Can I Build Strong Teams?

ASKING A GROUP TO WORK TOGETHER does not mean that you have created a team. In fact, there are major differences between a team and a group. A *group* consists of individuals who gather for a purpose (plan, vote, perform a task, play a game), to discuss issues, or to inform. A *team* builds on the group by defining roles for individual members, utilizing individual strengths, and nurturing synergies to create a unified plan of action to achieve identified results.

The Team-Building Process

Many teams are formed in organizations. These teams seem to be independent entities focused on solving problems or sharing information. However, it is important to be sure team members realize that their performance must align with the organization's goals. Team meetings without that understanding often end in discussion without a business outcome. The team-building process is a difficult one, but it will help if you keep the following points in mind:

1. Establish the team's purpose and its responsibility to the larger organization.

2. Discuss and agree on expected results; use consensus-seeking techniques, focusing on agreement rather than on disagreement.

3. Discuss the process, methods, and strategies that will lead to achieving goals.

4. Discuss and have each team member establish accountability within the team by accepting given roles. Discuss how each role will help the team succeed.

5. Recognize leaders, decision makers, and influencers by function, rather than by position.

6. Discuss and accept the team's process for communication (analytical, structured, random thoughts, big picture).

7. Create a safe environment to encourage trusting, open, honest, and respectful discussions.

8. Encourage individual perspectives, rather than promoting "group think" ("yes" people).

9. Continually foster rapport building among team members at meetings and social events.

10. Be willing to work through impasses to develop intellectual team growth.

11. Recognize individual achievement by team members to promote credibility and commitment.

12. Involve the entire team in the problem-solving and/or decision-making process by encouraging input and output from each team member.

13. Discuss ideas (content) and procedures (process) to lay the foundation for continual team building.

Stages of Group Development

Groups go through stages of development based on their composition and purpose. There are many models of team development. Although Tuckman's (1965) model: Forming (testing and dependence); Storming (conflict); Norming (team cohesion); and Performing (team productivity) may be the most well-known, here we will explore Charrier's (1974) model, which details the stages of development he calls "Cog's Ladder." Charrier's model identifies the maturing stages that a team goes through to become a viable and working entity. One way to measure the strength of a team is how it resolves conflict. The appearance of conflict usually indicates a more mature team, because very new teams are often uncomfortable surfacing conflict.

Charrier's Stages of Team Development

Stage 1. Polite Stage

- Members get to know one another.
- Members seek approval of authority figure.
- There is no conflict.
- There is no team identity.
- Information is exchanged politely.

Stage 2. Why Are We Here?

- There is focus on team goals.
- Cliques begin to develop.
- There is more participation.

Stage 3. Bid for Power

- The display of power, influence, and competence emerges.
- Conflict arises among cliques.
- Hidden agendas surface.
- The leader begins to emerge.

Stage 4. Construction

- Members listen and respond.
- Members show support for ideas and for one another.
- Leadership and followership are shared.

- Trust develops.
- Team engages in problem solving.

Stage 5. Development of Esprit

- Team loyalty surfaces.
- Cliques are eliminated.
- High trust is established.
- High productivity is developed.

All of the above stages are crucial to the development of an effective team. They define the character of the team, how the members will work with each other, and how they will achieve more collectively than as individuals.

Team Formation

The team's first task is to write a clearly worded purpose or mission statement that states its role within the organization and to identify its goals. What does it want to accomplish?

Second, the team must define members' roles. Each team member should discuss his or her strengths and how those strengths will contribute to the team's success.

Third, after roles are assigned, the team should create an action plan. This plan should lay out everyone's involvement and commitment. It should focus on the goals and take advantage of each member's strengths.

Team Growth

Team dynamics can have a mushrooming impact beyond merely goals attained or quotas met. Individual strengths will change as team members learn from one another and refine their processes. For this to happen, though, the members must build and shape a relationship based on openness, honesty, trust, and respect.

- *Openness* is speaking what you think rather than playing political games.

- *Honesty* is stating the facts clearly without purposeful ambiguity.
- *Trust* is being able to rely on one another.
- *Respect* is realizing that each person on the team deserves equal dignity.

Each team member contributes to the team's growth through these trusting, open, honest, and respectful communications. They do this in any of the many roles they perform as committed team members: informer, supporter, friend, supervisor, devil's advocate, innovator, representative, and so on. Together, these roles produce an environment that influences the team toward action.

Problems in Team Development

Developing individual roles and expectations within the team has advantages and disadvantages. When someone does not live up to the group's expectations—or vice versa—conflicts can occur. For instance, conflicts can occur when a member is perceived to exceed his or her role expectations or authority. The same is true if a member does *not* fulfill his or her responsibilities. The leader, for example, often has the most clearly defined role. If someone challenges the leader's expected role responsibility or authority, conflict may and often will occur.

Every team at some point will face barriers to success. Following are some typical problems found during team development that may affect the team adversely and some solutions to deal with these issues.

Problems	Solutions
Withdrawal/ self-censorship	Set Ground Rule 1: All members are equal parts of the team and must be involved.
Ideas rejected without consideration	Ground Rule 2: All ideas are worthy of consideration.

Problems	Solutions
Decisions made by upper management without team input	Ask management to give the team time to discuss policies before decisions are made.
Avoidance of decisions	Set a time frame for decisions on each issue and stick to it.
Feeling of "I am right because I am the leader"	Remind team of Ground Rule 1: All members are equal parts of the team.
Feelings of inadequacy	Tell team why you feel inadequate, because not all members have equal knowledge about all ideas.
Competition among team members	Remind team that its existence is built on teamwork, not on individuals.
Using poor listening skills	Ground Rule 3: All members must make a concerted effort to "listen without rebuttal."
Letting anger/disagreements fester	Ground Rule 4: Anger and disagreements must be worked out before moving on.
No support of risk taking	Don't make decisions NOT to fail, but rather make decisions to succeed.

List some ways that you might influence team members to avoid the common problems listed above.

Influencing As a Team Leader

One of the most influential roles you will play is that of a team leader. Your direction, guidance, control, and respect show others that you can be trusted and are worth listening to. There are several areas in which your influence will be especially important.

Create Expectations (Direction)

- What does the team want to accomplish? What are its mission statement, goals, and objectives?
- Identify the "why's" of the team (the team's responsibilities), and the "how's" (its processes) will fall into place.
- Set ground rules as to how the team will work together.
- Agree on reasonable results. Know what the team has done and when.

Work Together (Share Input)

- Promote an open, honest, trusting, and respectful relationship among all team members.
- Establish individual responsibilities.
- Set realistic time frames to accomplish the responsibilities.
- Give credit for jobs well done.
- Establish a way to discuss issues and work through problems.
- Learn to develop alternatives.

Organize (Set Priorities)

- Encourage team members to use their strengths to fulfill their team's responsibility.
- Avoid overlapping jobs.
- Don't reinvent the wheel; use what works well; learn from past experiences.

Act (Take the Right Action)

- Encourage each member's participation in meetings. Make sure there is balance; extroverts should quiet down, introverts should speak out.

- Remember to share what you feel safe and comfortable in sharing.
- Support each member's actions.
- Develop a plan of action and implement it.

Provide Closure (Summarize)

- Focus on what has been accomplished; recognize achievement.
- Identify follow-up action.

Overcoming "Group Think"

Gaining commitment or influencing others is difficult when team members strive for agreement and cohesiveness without expressing their feelings honestly—when everyone goes along to get along. This "group thinking" often occurs during stressful situations or changes, such as layoffs, budget cuts, or external pressure from competitors.

The problems associated with group thinking often manifest themselves in the following ways:

- *Illusion of Invulnerability.* This is the idea that if the entire group agrees, it will work.
- *Inherent Morality.* The members agree that they are the ones who are right.
- *Rationalization.* Because a solution seems appropriate and all agree, problems are downplayed or ignored.
- *Stereotyping of "Out" Groups.* This is the thought that because the group has special status, the members understand what needs to be done, but others do not (we/they feeling).
- *Self-Censorship.* This is someone making the assumption that the team may not agree, so he or she does not express thoughts and comments.
- *Direct Pressure.* The team leader indicates very strongly that only one solution will be accepted, and thus the leader forces the outcome.

- *Illusion of Unanimity.* Problems are downplayed, disagreements are frowned on, and agreement is forced.

To influence others in a difficult team setting, you'll have to call on your best communication and collaboration skills. As the group moderator, you'll want to do the following:

- Encourage open, free, and nondefensive discussions.
- Collect input from people outside the team.
- Allow people to evaluate issues without fear of criticism.
- Avoid directing. Be flexible and guide the team to meet its needs.

RESOURCES

Charrier, G. (1974). Cog's ladder: A model of group development. In J.E. Jones & J.W. Pfeiffer (Eds.), *The 1974 annual handbook for group facilitators* (pp. 142–145). San Francisco, CA: Jossey-Bass/Pfeiffer.

Gatto, R. (1992). *Teamwork through flexible leadership.* Pittsburgh, PA: GTA Press.

Humphrey, B., & Stokes, J. (1997). *Teamguides: A self-directed system for teams.* San Francisco, CA: Jossey-Bass/Pfeiffer.

Janis, I.L. (1982). *Groupthink: Psychological studies of policy decisions and fiascoes* (2nd ed.). Boston, MA: Houghton Mifflin.

Kayser, T.A. (1994). *Team power: How to unleash the collaborative genius of work teams.* New York: Irwin.

Phillips, S., & Elledge, R. (1989). *The team-building sourcebook.* San Francisco, CA: Jossey-Bass/Pfeiffer.

Rees, F. (1991). *How to lead work teams.* San Francisco, CA: Jossey-Bass/Pfeiffer.

Rees, F. (1997). *Teamwork from start to finish.* San Francisco, CA: Jossey-Bass/Pfeiffer.

Richards, D., & Smyth, S. (1994). *Assessing your team: 7 measures of team success.* San Francisco, CA: Jossey-Bass/Pfeiffer.

Tuckman, B.W. (1965). Development sequences in small groups. *Psychological Bulletin, 63,* 384–399.

Wellins, R.S., Byham, W.C., & Wilson, J.M. (1991). *Empowered teams.* San Francisco, CA: Jossey-Bass.

Q What Can I Do to Help My Team Communicate Better?

EFFECTIVE COMMUNICATION is the key that opens all doors, because how an idea is presented and received is the key factor to success. Because teams are likely to be composed of members with different speaking and listening styles, it is important to lay some ground rules so that all team members have the opportunity both to contribute and to hear others' ideas. When presenting ideas, ask the team members to adhere to the following ground rules:

- The idea should be stated clearly.
- The idea should contribute to, not detract from, the topic at hand.
- The team leader is responsible for encouraging open and honest discussion and for directing the discussion of ideas to a successful conclusion.
- The team should encourage debate between its members in a safe environment to promote a well-thought-out plan of action that will accomplish the expected results.

The following list illustrates the different tasks the leader performs when working with a team:

- Creates a direction for the team by refining and clearly stating the goals.
- Shares information in depth with all members of the team via frequent meetings.
- Obtains input from all team members, stipulating that all ideas are valuable and worth consideration.
- Focuses on task and how to work together effectively.
- Sets meeting agendas and time schedules and relays such information to all team members.
- Prioritizes work of the team; reaches consensus with team members as to task priorities.
- Assumes a responsible role for the success of the team and communicates this to the team members.
- Secures commitment to stated goals from all members of the team.
- Reaches team agreement on actions before taking such actions.
- Takes the actions supported by the team; talks to management, sends memos, presents proposed actions.

Team Process Evaluation

If you are currently on a team, you can evaluate how effectively it is performing by completing this brief exercise. Put a "P" at the point on each of the following continuum lines that best describes the team's *Present* functioning.

Team acts too quickly	There is a good balance between discussion and action	Team discusses too long; takes little action

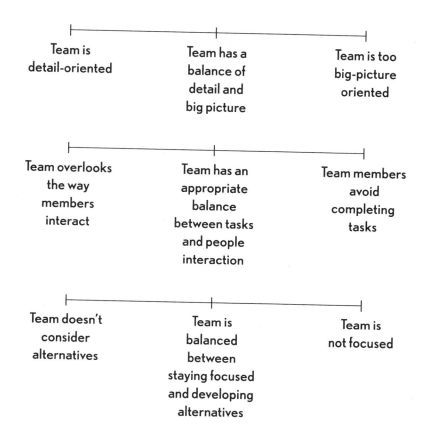

Team is detail-oriented | Team has a balance of detail and big picture | Team is too big-picture oriented

Team overlooks the way members interact | Team has an appropriate balance between tasks and people interaction | Team members avoid completing tasks

Team doesn't consider alternatives | Team is balanced between staying focused and developing alternatives | Team is not focused

By completing this little exercise, you will have a good idea of how well your team performs at the present time. If your four P's are centered on the continuum lines, your team is functioning well. If your P's are more to the left margin, your team is probably functioning more as a group of individuals rather than as a team and is more concerned with expediency than effectiveness. If your P's are more to the right margin, your team may be mired in the process and unable or unwilling to produce solutions.

It is evident that team communication is an essential function. Each of the four descriptors of the balance a team leader must maintain (between discussion and action, detail and big picture, tasks and people interaction, and focusing and developing alternatives) is critical to team function. Without effective communication and the ability to follow through, a team is simply a group of individuals who happen to be in the same place at the same time.

RESOURCES

Argyris, C. (1994). Good communication that blocks learning. *Harvard Business Review, 72*(4), 77–85.

Bion, W.R. (1959). *Experiences in groups.* New York: Basic Books.

Gatto, R. (1992). *Teamwork through flexible leadership.* Pittsburgh, PA: GTA Press.

Knowles, M., & Knowles, H. (1972). *Introduction to group dynamics.* Upper Saddle River, NJ: Prentice Hall.

Luft, J. (1984). *Group processes: An introduction to group dynamics* (3rd ed.). San Francisco, CA: Mayfield.

Stewart, G.L., Manz, C.C., & Sims, H.P. (1999). *Teamwork and group dynamics.* New York: Wiley.

Time
Management

Q How Can I Evaluate How I Spend My Time?

FROM THE DAY YOU START kindergarten you are concerned with time. The one educational concept that is practically universal is *to be on time*. Today's society is filled with deadlines and ultimatums. How well you meet those time constraints is one indicator of your success. Your success may have nothing to do with intelligence, ability, or skill—it simply indicates how well you manage time.

Time management is the effective utilization of time to complete daily duties and long-term projects efficiently. Time may be managed in part by establishing priorities, maintaining a schedule (short- or long-term), and developing alternatives to deal with change. Following are some suggestions for improving your time-management skills.

1. At the start of each day, spend five to ten minutes writing a plan of action. This can lessen daily stress by helping you to visualize your day and to develop a schedule in writing. A sample daily planner (with a few filled-in samples) follows.

Sample Daily Planner

Date: _____

Meeting	Time	Place
_____	_____	_____
_____	_____	_____
_____	_____	_____
_____	_____	_____

Calls to Make	Call-Backs
_____	_____
_____	_____
_____	_____
_____	_____

Tasks	Time Requirements	Issues
1. *Call Purchasing*	*10 minutes*	*Do they expect shipment on time?*
2. *Meet with reps*	*10:00 a.m. to 11 a.m.*	*Review new policy*
3.		
4.		

2. As the day progresses, write down any additional work or projects that need to be completed. Review the list at the end of the day and add unfinished business to the next day's plan. Give yourself credit for what you have accomplished.

3. Outline projects. Indicate purpose, expected results, and level of importance (urgent, important, not urgent, or unimportant). Include these topic areas:

   Expect to accomplish

   Associates involved

   Equipment needed

   Date of completion

   Need to inform

   Need to meet with

   Possible in-house problems

   Possible customer/client problems

   Using this outline will help you focus your thoughts, clarify directions, and establish a procedure for working.

4. Develop alternatives for accomplishing your priority responsibilities efficiently. For example, establish a time period each day when you take no interruptions and focus on a priority.

5. Develop a system for giving information and receiving feedback, such as an informal ten-minute meeting each morning.

6. Make sure each involved associate, supervisor, and/or manager knows his or her role and the project deadlines.

7. Analyze your greatest time problems; plan for them and develop alternatives. Following are some typical work-related time problems:

   - Interruptions—phone calls, unexpected visitors, and so forth.

   - Organizational issues—not knowing who does what; not knowing the amount of time or number of associates needed to accomplish priority responsibilities.

- Time on task—not knowing how long it will take associates or supervisor/management to accomplish responsibilities. Remember, time spent on task does not ensure quality.

- Gathering information—not knowing how to collect, share, and disseminate data.

- Lack of supervision—a person must first manage himself or herself in order to meet expectations. A manager's responsibility is to lead, not to perform an associate's job. If a supervisor is not providing direction, time could be lost. Internal conflict can arise from a managerial attitude of "I can do the job better than other associates." If you as the manager take on everyone else's responsibilities, your job will not be done. Know how and when to delegate.

- Emergencies/crises—the unexpected happens (equipment failure, associate absences, and so forth).

- Associate problems—associates not fulfilling expectations, doing much more than is needed to obtain results, or duplicating work of others.

- Meetings—essential, yet time-consuming. Poorly planned meetings mean essential topics aren't discussed and time is wasted.

- Nonessential work—job responsibilities that are not high priority but that need to be accomplished.

8. Regular meetings may be essential to complete job responsibilities within a given time frame. Updates of what has been and what needs to be accomplished should be discussed. Prepare an agenda, discuss only pertinent issues, and do not extend the meeting longer than necessary.

9. Send out FYI (for your information) memos. Use simple graphics and diagrams whenever possible because they

give the reader a "quick hit" of information. Sharing information is often the key to success. Everyone needs the same information to do his or her job well and on time.

To-Do and I Did Lists

In addition to a daily planner, many people also utilize to-do lists. As you think of a responsibility or task, write it on a to-do list. At the end of each day many people look at a to-do list and check off what they have accomplished. Instead, try creating an "I did" list at the end of the day (a sample follows). There are many things that you do that were unplanned (phone calls, interruptions by others), yet you provided a service. Give yourself credit for the services you provide, tasks you accomplish, and deadlines you meet.

Compare your to-do list with the "I did" list. This will give you better insight into what you need to do tomorrow and what you have accomplished today. When you look at your "I did" list at the end of a day, you will realize all you have accomplished. This can give you a sense of fulfillment, rather than having a sense of despair when looking only at the to-do list.

Sample "I Did" List

1. Action | Service Provided | Outcome
Purchasing called | *Gave specific* | *Will let me know*
| *measurements* | *by Tuesday if there*
| *for steel needed* | *will be a delay.*
| *for project.* |

2. Action | Service Provided | Outcome

3. Action	Service Provided	Outcome

4. Action	Service Provided	Outcome

Keys to Productivity

- Set realistic, productive goals.
- Have a place in which you always keep your to-do list.
- Think—organize—act.
- Focus on priorities.
- Define daily destinations.
- Don't compete.
- Don't waste time in unorganized events.
- Focus on your own work, not on others.'
- Maintain an even energy flow for yourself.

Analyzing the Work Day

Another tool for time management is the Work Day Analysis. Consider your normal work week. Do you know how much time you spend on various activities? If not, make a list of your major activities (most people have between six and ten) and keep notes on how you spend your time for the next week. Record the time in ten-minute sections. A sample Work Day Analysis for a typical week follows.

Sample Work Day Analysis

Activity	Ten Minute Segments		Total Minutes
Replying to mail	‖‖‖ ‖‖‖ ‖‖‖ ‖‖‖ ‖‖‖ ‖‖‖ ‖‖‖ ‖‖‖ ‖‖‖ ‖‖‖ ‖‖‖ ‖‖‖ ‖‖‖ ‖	(66)	660
Telephone calls	‖‖‖ ‖‖‖ ‖‖‖ ‖‖‖ ‖‖‖	(24)	240
Handling crises	‖‖‖ ‖‖‖ ‖‖‖ ‖‖‖ ‖‖	(22)	220
Interruptions	‖‖‖ ‖‖‖ ‖‖‖ ‖‖‖ ‖	(21)	210
Initiating/planning	‖‖‖ ‖‖‖ ‖‖‖ ‖‖‖ ‖‖	(22)	220
Talking with boss/peers	‖‖‖ ‖‖‖ ‖‖‖ ‖	(16)	160
Attending meetings	‖‖‖ ‖‖‖ ‖‖‖ ‖‖‖	(18)	180
Computer time	‖‖‖ ‖‖‖	(10)	100
Seeing visitors	‖‖‖ ‖‖‖ ‖‖‖ ‖‖‖	(19)	190
Other	‖‖‖ ‖‖‖ ‖‖‖ ‖‖‖ ‖‖	(22)	220
Total			2400

The following is a blank diary form for you to use.

Activity	Ten Minute Segments	Total Minutes
1. _____	_____	_____
2. _____	_____	_____
3. _____	_____	_____
4. _____	_____	_____
5. _____	_____	_____
6. _____	_____	_____
7. _____	_____	_____
8. _____	_____	_____
9. _____	_____	_____
10. _____	_____	_____
Total		_____

Another way to show how you have spent your time is to divide a circle, representing the full week, according to how you spent your time. A typical example for an administrator is shown here.

After you have had a chance to track your activities for a week, complete your own chart on the form below and then answer the review questions about your week. It should be instructive.

Review Questions

Examine your chart and answer the following questions about your week. These questions are meant to stimulate thought and discussion. Ask others to help you find practical ways for using your time more creatively and productively.

1. How can I react less and initiate more?

2. How can I spend less time fighting fires?

3. How can I use meeting time more productively?

4. How can I cut down on interruptions?

5. Was personal time spent for work?

6. Which of my activities were actually lower priorities?

7. Are the physical arrangements of my workplace conducive to optimum use of my time?

8. On whom or what am I spending too much of my time?

9. On whom or what am I spending too little of my time?

10. What major problem is apparent from my chart?

11. What ideas have others given me for improving my use of time?

12. Where do my attempts to improve my use of time generally fail?

Controlled Versus Uncontrolled Time

Another way to analyze how you spent your time is to look at the *effectiveness* of how you spend your time. There are two ways to look at time: controlled and uncontrolled.

Controlled time is time that is completely under your own control. You have the discretion of how you will use the time. *Uncontrolled*, or reactive, time is spent at the demand of others: the telephone rings, your boss drops in, or an employee stops by to ask questions. If too much of the work day is spent by using uncontrolled time, your productivity may slip. You may also be the victim of any of these:

- Distractions;
- Interruptions;
- Endless meetings; and/or
- Work overload because you can't get to it.

Controlling Your Time

To get a handle on how you control your time, establish a balance between controlled and uncontrolled time. Fill in the following chart with your daily work activities and the amount of time each takes. You may want to choose a particular day and fill out the chart as the activities occur. At the end of the day, decide whether each activity was an example of controlled time use or uncontrolled/reactive time use.

Activity	Total Hours	Controlled	Uncontrolled	Comment
Reading				
Telephone & Voice Mail				
Lunch, Breaks				
Crises				
Interruptions				
Planning				
Drop-Ins				
Meetings				
Computer Time, E-Mail				
Unproductive Time (Social)				
Boss's Needs				
Assisting Co-Workers				
Correspondence				
Other				

Mismanagement of time is frequently due to one of the following:

- Mismanagement of communication; lack of focus on agreement;
- Mismanagement of work load;
- Mismanagement of interruptions (always plan for interruptions);
- Lack of agreement on expectations and no clarity on what is to be accomplished;
- Lack of asserting your own viewpoint; not wanting to take a risk; or
- Not paying attention to where times goes; not controlling the time you can control.

After considering whether any of these are affecting your use of time, using the chart on the following page, make a list of your controlled versus your uncontrolled activities and the amount of time each took.

To be flexible and be able to meet the changes in a work day, plan on being in control of about half of your day. In other words, protect at least half of your time to accomplish what you want and need to do. Then when you make a to-do list, factor in how much time you will actually have to accomplish each activity. The following exercise will help you focus what you have learned about managing your time.

Controlled Activities	Amount of Time Taken	Uncontrolled Activities	Amount of Time Taken

Analyzing Your Time

After reviewing your assessments of how you spend your time, record your responses to the following questions.

1. Which part of each day was most productive? Which was least productive? Why?

2. What were the recurring patterns of efficiency and of inefficiency in your days?

3. What do you do that may not be necessary? What is necessary that you did not do?

4. How could you eliminate some of your uncontrolled time activities?

5. How can you turn your uncontrolled time activities into controlled time activities? List some specific uncontrolled activities and think about how to change them.

   Activity 1:

   Activity 2:

   Activity 3:

Improving Your
Time Management Skills

To control your time successfully, focus on the following and make a few notes on what each means for you:

- What needs to be achieved—the goals and results;

- Performance standards;

- The big picture, not minute-to-minute changes;

- Prioritizing interactions and requests by associates and organizational authorities; and

- The tradeoff for performing one task versus another task.

Summary

Now that you have finished reviewing some tools for managing your time, your real challenge begins: systematically implementing and applying what you have learned. If you utilize the tools from this chapter, including the Daily Planner, to-do and "I did" lists, the Work Day Analysis, and others, you will discover that you can begin to manage time more effectively.

RESOURCES

Gatto, R. (1999). *Time management workbook.* Unpublished manuscript. Gatto Training Associates, 733 Washington Road, Pittsburgh, PA 15228.

Gibson, J., Ivancevich, J., & Donnelly, J. (1997). *Organizations.* Boston, MA: Irwin/McGraw-Hill.

Haynes, M. (1994). *Personal time management.* Menlo Park, CA: Crisp.

Schultz, D., & Schultz, S. (1998). *Psychology and work today* (7th ed.). Upper Saddle River, NJ: Prentice Hall.

 **Additional Resources**

Albrecht, K., & Zemke, R. (1985). *Service America!* Homewood, IL: Dow Jones-Irwin.

Alderfer, C. (1972). *Existence, relatedness and growth.* New York: The Free Press.

Argyris, C. (1973). *Intervention theory and method: A behavioral science view.* Reading, MA: Addison-Wesley.

Baron, R.A., & Greenberg, J. (1986). *Behavior in organizations.* Boston, MA: Allyn and Bacon.

Bass, B. (1981). *Stogdill's handbook of leadership.* New York: The Free Press.

Bass, B. (1985). *Leadership and performance beyond expectations.* New York: The Free Press.

Bellach, A., & Hersen, M. (1988). *Behavioral assessment.* New York: Pergamon Press.

Bennis, W. (1989). Why leaders can't lead: The unconscious conspiracy continuum. San Francisco, CA: Jossey-Bass.

Bennis, W., & Nanus, B. (1985). *Leaders: The strategy for taking charge.* New York: Harper and Row.

Bion, W.R. (1959). *Experiences in group.* New York: Basic Books.

Blanchard, K., Zigarmi, P., & Zygarmi, D. (1985). *Leadership and the one minute manager*. New York: William Morrow.

Bryant, G. (1984). *The working women report*. New York: Simon and Schuster.

Burns, D. (1989). *The feeling good handbook*. New York: Plume Books.

Carnegie, D., & Associates. (1993). *The leader in you*. New York: Simon and Schuster.

Champagne, D., & Hogan, C. (1981). *Consultant supervision theory and skill development*. Pittsburgh, PA: Author.

Charrier, G. (1974). *Cog's ladder: A model of group development*. In J.E. Jones & J.W. Pfeiffer (Eds.), *The 1974 annual handbook for group facilitators* (pp. 142–145). San Francisco, CA: Jossey-Bass/Pfeiffer.

Covey, S. (1989). *The seven habits of highly effective people*. New York: Simon and Schuster.

Deep, S., & Sussman, L. (1990). *Smart moves*. Reading, MA: Addison-Wesley.

De Pree, M. (1988). *Leadership is an art*. New York: Dell.

Drucker, P. (1954). *The practice of management*. New York: Harper and Row.

Drucker, P. (1964). *Managing for results*. New York: Harper and Row.

Drucker, P. (1989). *The new realities*. New York: Harper and Row.

Dunnette, M. (1976). *Educational handbook of industrial and organizational psychology*. Chicago, IL: Rand-McNally.

Egan, G. (1986). *The skilled helper: A systematic approach to effective helping*. Belmont, CA: Brooks/Cole.

Eitzen, D. (1978). *In conflict and order: Understanding society*. Boston, MA: Allyn and Bacon.

Ellis, A., & Lange, A. (1994). *How to keep people from pushing your buttons*. New York: Carol Publishing Group.

Freeman, A., & DeWolf, R. (1989). *Woulda coulda shoulda*. New York: Silver Arrow.

Gatto, R. (1985). *Learning styles based curriculum: Left brain/right brain dominance. Achievement motivation and success*. Washington, DC: Educational Leadership Council of America.

Gatto, R. (1990). *A practical guide to effective presentation*. Pittsburgh, PA: GTA Press.

Gatto, R. (1991). *Controlling stress in the workplace*. Pittsburgh, PA: GTA Press.

Gatto, R. (1992). *Teamwork through flexible leadership*. Pittsburgh, PA: GTA Press.

Gatto, R. (1995). *Reflections from the workplace.* Pittsburgh, PA: GTA Press.

Gibson, J., Ivancevich, J., & Donnelly, J. (1997). *Organizations.* Boston, MA: Irwin/McGraw-Hill.

Greenberg, J. (1999). *Managing behavior in organizations.* Upper Saddle River, NJ: Prentice Hall.

Grief, B., & Munter, P. (1980). *Tradeoffs: Executive family and organizational life.* New York: New American Library.

Hall, J. (1988). *Models of management: The structure of competence.* The Woodlands, TX: Woodstead Press.

Hammer, M., & Champy, J. (1993). *Reengineering the corporation.* New York: HarperCollins.

Hertzberg, F. (1966, September). One more time: How do you motivate employees? *Harvard Business Review,* pp. 1–10.

Hertzberg, F. (1966). *Work and nature of man.* Cleveland, OH: World Publishing.

Holmes, T.H., & Rahe, R.H. (1967). Social readjustment rating scale. *Journal of Psychosomatic Research, 11,* 213–218.

Juran, J. (1989). *Juran on leadership for quality.* New York: The Free Press.

Karp, H. (1985). *Personal power: An unorthodox guide to success.* New York: American Management Association.

Knowles, J. (1975). *Self-directed learning.* New York: Cambridge.

Knowles, M. (1980). *Modern practice of adult education.* Chicago, IL: Follett.

Knowles, M. (1984). *The adult learner—A neglected species.* Houston, TX: Gulf.

Knowles, M., & Knowles, H. (1972). *Introduction to group dynamics.* Upper Saddle River, NJ: Cambridge Adult Education.

Lawless, D. (1979). *Organizational behavior: The psychology of effective management.* Upper Saddle River, NJ: Prentice Hall.

Learning Annex. (1984). *How to win on the telephone.* New York: Berkley Books.

Lowan, R. (1998). *The ethical practice of psychology in organizations.* Washington, DC: American Psychological Association.

Lutherans, F. (1998). *Organizational behavior.* Boston, MA: Irwin/McGraw-Hill.

Mahler, W. (1975). *Structure, power and results.* Homewood, IL: Dow Jones-Irwin.

Maslow, A. (1970). *Motivation on personality* (2nd ed.). New York: Harper and Row.

Maslow, A. (1970). *The farther reaches of human nature*. New York: Viking Press.

Matteson, M.T., & Ivancevich, J.M. (1983). Note on tension discharge rate as an employee health status predictor. *Academy of Management Journal, 26,* 540–545.

May, R. (1989). *The art of counseling*. New York: Gardner Press.

McClelland, D. (1965, November/December). Achievement motivation can be developed. *Harvard Business Review,* pp. 64–70.

McClelland, D., & Burnham, D. (1976, March/April). Power is the great motivator. *Harvard Business Review.*

Mussen, P., Conger, J., Kogan, J., & Geiwitz, J. (1979). *Psychological development: A life span approach*. New York: Harper and Row.

Nierenberg, G. (1982). *The art of creative thinking*. New York: Cornerstone Library.

Ornstein, R. (1972). *The psychology of consciousness*. New York: Penguin Books.

Ostrander, S., & Schroeder, L. (1979). *Superlearning*. New York: Delacorte.

Peters, T. (1987). *Thriving on chaos*. New York: Alfred A. Knopf.

Peters, T., & Waterman, R., Jr. (1982). *In search of excellence*. New York: Harper and Row.

Porter, L., Lawler, E., & Hachman, R. (1975). *Behavior in organizations*. New York: McGraw-Hill.

Schultz, D., & Schultz, S.E. (1998). *Psychology and work today*. Upper Saddle River, NJ: Prentice Hall.

Selye, H. (Ed.). (1980). *Selye's guide to stress research* (Vol. 1). New York: Van Nostrand Reinhold.

Shaw, J.B., & Riskind, P. (1983). Predicting job stress using data from the position analysis questionnaire. *Journal of Applied Psychology, 68,* 253–261.

Springer, S., & Deutsch, G. (1981). *Left brain right brain*. San Francisco, CA: W.H. Freeman.

Tuckman, B.W. (1965). Developmental sequence in small groups. *Psychological Bulletin, 63,* 384–399.

Von Oech, R. (1992). *A whack on the side of the head*. Menlo Park, CA: Creative Thinking.

Yeomans, W. (1985). *1000 things you never learned in business school*. New York: McGraw-Hill.

About the Author

REX P. GATTO is founder and president of Gatto Training Associates (GTA). His practice has been dedicated to helping people in the workplace to enhance productivity through a better understanding of themselves. He has done extensive research in the areas of individual working, thinking, personality, leadership, teamwork, and communication styles and their impact on the working environment. As a behavioral scientist and counselor, he has devoted his energies to helping all levels of business people—CEO's, vice presidents, managers, and professionals—to have an enriched work life. He consults on matters of organizational effectiveness, conducts training programs, and also conducts one-on-one and group counseling.

Gatto holds undergraduate and master's degrees in education from Duquesne University, a master of arts in counseling psychology from Norwich University, a Ph.D. from the University of Pittsburgh, and Pennsylvania certifications as an educator and supervisor of curriculum and instruction. He is board certified as a national certified counselor (NCC) and cognitive therapist and a nationally certified psychologist.

He has written five books: *A Practical Guide to Effective Presentation, Controlling Stress in the Workplace, Teamwork Through Flexible Leadership, Reflections from the Workplace,* and *The Answers to Frequently Asked Questions from the Workplace.* The books are based on his years of experience working with businesspeople throughout the United States and Canada.

He has written training manuals and developed assessment instruments specifically for people within the workplace. The list of training manual topics includes leadership development, effective presentations, stress management, sales, effective listening, professional development, team building, support staff development, meeting leadership, supervisory and management development, problem solving, employee assessment, creativity, and positive influence. In the area of employee assessment, he has developed inventories on interpersonal working associations, communication, self-directed achievement (performance management), listening skills, leadership performance, customer/client profile, motivation, teamwork, and manager assessment simulations.

Gatto is a member of the following organizations: American Psychological Association, Pennsylvania Psychological Association, Society for Industrial and Organizational Psychology, American Counseling Association, Pennsylvania Counseling Association, and American Society for Training and Development.

He can be reached via his website, *www.rexgatto.com.*